A
CONSERVATIONIST
MANIFESTO

Also by Scott Russell Sanders

NONFICTION

A Private History of Awe
The Force of Spirit
The Country of Language
Hunting for Hope
Writing from the Center
Staying Put
Secrets of the Universe
The Paradise of Bombs
In Limestone Country

FICTION

The Invisible Company
The Engineer of Beasts
Bad Man Ballad
Terrarium
Wonders Hidden
Fetching the Dead
Hear the Wind Blow
Wilderness Plots

SCOTT RUSSELL SANDERS

A

CONSERVATIONIST MANIFESTO

Indiana University Press
Bloomington & Indianapolis

This book is a publication of
Indiana University Press
601 North Morton Street
Bloomington, IN 47404-3797 USA

http://iupress.indiana.edu

Telephone orders	800-842-6796
Fax orders	812-855-7931
Orders by e-mail	iuporder@indiana.edu

The author warmly thanks the editors of the following publications, in which earlier versions of the essays contained in this book first appeared: "Building Arks" under the title "A Fleet of Arks" in *Wild Earth* and *Resurgence;* "Common Wealth" in *Tikkun;* "A Few Earthy Words" in Helen Whybrow, ed., *The Story Handbook: Language and Storytelling for Land Conservationists* (San Francisco: The Trust for Public Land, 2002); "Two Stones" in *The Louisville Review;* "The Warehouse and the Wilderness" in *Water-Stone;* "The Geography of Somewhere" as Foreword to Dan Shilling, *Civic Tourism: The Poetry and Politics of Place* (Prescott, Arizona: Sharlott Hall Museum Press, 2007); "Hometown" under the title "Where Belonging Is a Virtue" in *Notre Dame Magazine;* "On Loan from the Sundance Sea" in *Preservation;* "Big Trees, Still Water, Tall Grass" in Barry Lopez, ed., *Heart of a Nation: Writers and Photographers Inspired by the American Landscape* (Washington, D.C.: National Geographic Society, 2000); "Limberlost" under the title "Limberlost and Found" in *Audubon;* "Wilderness as a Sabbath for the Land" in Hank Lentfer and Carolyn Servid, eds., *Arctic Refuge: A Circle of Testimony* (Minneapolis, MN: Milkweed Editions, March 2001) and, expanded, in *Spiritus;* "Simplicity and Sanity" in *The Georgia Review;* "Stillness" in *Orion;* "A Conservationist Manifesto" in Helen Whybrow, ed., *Coming to Land in a Troubled World* (San Francisco: The Trust for Public Land, 2003); "For the Children" under the title "A Letter to Tomorrow" in *Notre Dame Magazine.*

Manufactured in the United States of America

Library of Congress Cataloging-in-Publication Data

Sanders, Scott R. (Scott Russell), date-
A conservationist manifesto / Scott Russell Sanders.
p. cm.
Includes bibliographical references.
ISBN 978-0-253-35313-9 (cloth : alk. paper) — ISBN 978-0-253-22080-6 (pbk. : alk. paper)
1. Nature conservation—United States. I. Title.

QH76.S26 2009
333.72—dc22

2008039531

2 3 4 5   14 13 12 11 10 09

FOR PETER FORBES AND HELEN WHYBROW

Among all creatures, we are the only kind
that frets, the only kind that asks forgiveness,
or needs to. Meanwhile, crows palaver
in the pines, crickets sing in the high grass,
cottonwoods wag their leaves in every least wind.

Having held our tongues to listen, having fallen asleep
to the barred owl's call and wakened to fog over the Mad
River, having seen the pond shiver like the taut hide
of a horse and the dew ignite with dawn, freed now to break
silence, we might find words to speak our love of Earth.

After you have exhausted what there is
in business, politics, conviviality, love,
and so on—have found that none of these
finally satisfy, or permanently wear—
what remains?
Nature remains; to bring out
from their torpid recesses,
the affinities of a man or woman
with the open air, the trees, fields,
the changes of seasons—the sun by day
and the stars of heaven by night.
We will begin from these convictions.

WALT WHITMAN

Contents

Preface

Trapped recently in an airport lounge where there was no escape from television, I saw an advertisement that showed a husband and wife in an electronics store rushing from one gadget to another, their eyes agog with desire, their mouths curled into rapturous grins, while a chorus of voices chanted, "I want it all, and I want it now!"

This expression of unbridled appetite, neatly combining gluttony and impatience, might stand as the motto for our commercial culture. The same impulse prompts children to throw tantrums when their parents refuse to buy them candy or sneakers or toys. Most of us, I suspect, think of such children as spoiled. Yet the ad implies that once we are grown up and equipped with charge cards, we no longer need to throw tantrums, for we can have everything we want, without pain or delay. Politicians echo this appeal to our gluttony by promising to cut taxes while offering us more handouts and services. Technologists indulge our impatience by peddling gadgets that will let us do everything faster, regardless of whether what we're doing is worth doing at all. Merchants and media, pollsters and pundits, agree in defining us as consumers, as if the purpose of life were to devour the world rather than to savor and preserve it.

As an antidote to this culture of consumption, extravagance, and waste that dominates America today, we need to imagine a culture of conservation. The reasons are manifold. Whether one considers the disruption of global climate, the tattering of the ozone layer, the clear-cutting of forests, the loss of topsoil, the poisoning of lakes by acid rain, the collapse of ocean fisheries, the extinction of species, the looming shortages of oil and fresh water, the spread of famine and epidemic disease, or dozens of other challenges, it's clear that our present way of life is ruinous for the planet and for all Earth's creatures.

How might we shift to a more durable and responsible way of life? What models do we have for a culture of conservation? What changes in values and behavior would be required to bring it about? Where can we see it emerging in practice?

This book seeks answers to those questions. Ranging geographically from my home ground in southern Indiana to the Mount St. Helens volcano and Alaska's Glacier Bay and Minnesota's Boundary Waters Wilderness, and ranging culturally from the Bible to billboards, it maps the practical, ecological, and ethical grounds for a conservation ethic. The roots of conservation go deep in America, back through such visionaries as Rachel Carson, Aldo Leopold, John Muir, and Henry David Thoreau; back through the frugal habits of the Depression and wartime rationing, through agrarian thrift and frontier ingenuity and the prudent advice of Poor Richard's Almanack; back through Quakers and Puritans, with their emphasis on material simplicity; and even farther back to the indigenous people who inhabited this continent before it was called America.

This tradition of living modestly and conservingly has been largely eclipsed in our own day. While comprising less than 5 percent of the world's population, Americans account for some 25 percent of the world's use of nonrenewable resources, and the amounts we use are increasing year by year. We likewise account for roughly 25 percent of the world's annual release of greenhouse gases. Yet in 2001, the vice president of the United States remarked that "Conservation may be

CHENEY

a sign of personal virtue, but it is not a sufficient basis for a sound, comprehensive energy policy." In 2006, when a former vice president called on the United States to freeze our greenhouse gas emissions at their current levels and then begin reducing them, the chair of the Senate Environment and Public Works Committee responded that any such limitation on growth would cause an "economic calamity." The senator did not acknowledge, or perhaps even know, that our economic behavior is already causing an ecological calamity.

This book argues that the practice of conservation is not merely a "personal virtue." It is the most public of virtues, an expression of our regard for our neighbors, for this marvelous planet, and for future generations.

Over the past five years, my wife and I have become grandparents three times over, through the births of Elizabeth Rachel Allen and Margaret Lys Allen to our daughter, Eva, and her husband, Matthew, and through the birth of Anna Katharine Sanders to our son, Jesse, and his wife, Carrie. If I were ever in danger of forgetting why we should preserve Earth's bounty and beauty, these children remind me.

PART
1

Caring for Earth

Building Arks

*I*n muggy July, police showed up at dawn with bullhorns, bulldozers, chainsaws, and guns to force a band of protesters out of a fifty-acre wood in my hometown of Bloomington, Indiana. The sheriff and his deputies and the state police were upholding a ruling by the county council, which gave an Indianapolis developer the right to turn these woods into an apartment complex. The protesters were upholding the right of the woods to remain a woods, one of the last parcels of big trees left within the noose of roads that encircles our city. A few protesters had lived for months up in the trees on makeshift platforms, while local people took turns bringing them food and drink. The tree-sitters were arrested along with a number of their supporters, sixteen in all, and they are now awaiting trial. As I write these lines, the trees are falling, and a private security firm guards the perimeter of the vanishing woods.

The police had the law on their side, of course, but they also had the banks, building contractors, realtors, truck drivers, merchants, utility companies, fast-food vendors, city newspaper, and countless other boosters that stood to make money from the development. The protesters set against that power their unarmed bodies and their unfashionable convictions. They believe there are values more important than money. They believe that red oaks and red foxes and all the creatures of the woods deserve a home. They believe that a civilized community must show restraint by leaving some land alone, to remind us of the wild world on which our lives depend and to keep us humble and sane.

Similar conflicts are being played out from coast to coast, in more or less dramatic fashion, over the fate of more or fewer acres. By and large the boosters are winning. The U.S. Department of Agriculture estimates that we are losing 2.2 million acres of open space to development each year, including farms, forests, wetlands, and prairies. I will return to my own local struggle later on, but first I need to place it within a larger frame. So bear with me. I must begin by speaking of the trouble we're in before I can say how we might get out of it.

It's plain that Earth cannot support for much longer the extravagant way of life so common in rich countries, nor can it support the spreading of that extravagance to poor countries. Sooner or later we'll burn up all the cheap oil, we'll pump the aquifers dry, we'll cut down the last big trees, we'll fish the oceans bare, we'll plow up the last arable land, and taint the last clean air. The life of endless consumption is devastating to the planet and bound to fail. The question is not whether it will fail but when, and how the end of our spree will come—by careful preparation, or by catastrophe.

Knowing all this, how should a person act? We might shrug off the knowledge, pretend we can go on building vast houses, driving enormous cars, shopping around the clock, wiping out other species, fouling the atmosphere, polluting water, and squandering soil forever and ever. We might admit the gravity of our situation, while counting on scientists and engineers to come up with a technical fix. We might place our faith in the free market, believing it will somehow furnish a second, unspoiled Earth for our use, once the price is right. We might concede that neither economics nor technology will enable us to pursue infinite growth on a finite globe, and so decide to live it up while we can, leaving future generations to figure out how to survive on a ransacked planet. Or we might seek to live more lightly, reducing our demands on Earth, devising or recovering simple, elegant, durable practices that could serve our descendants long after the current binge of consumption has withered away.

The first four responses to Earth's limits are by far the most visible. Many people refuse to see the abundant signs that the fabric of life is fraying. They simply deny that there is any reason for concern, and the more the evidence piles up, the louder their denials. Others believe in technology, trusting that genetic engineering, fuel cells, molecular machines, missile shields, or some other stratagem will spare us from having to curtail our numbers or our desires. Others trust in the magic of the market to overcome limits, as if the mechanism that got us into this dead-end way of life will somehow get us out, if only we will apply it more fervently. Still others, and perhaps the majority, know that we are living on borrowed time, that Earth's reserves are running out, and yet they go on gobbling up toys and sensations anyway. They don't apologize for their gluttony, and they don't lie awake nights pondering where it might lead.

By comparison, those who strive to live more simply are harder to see. They don't crowd the malls or the fast food shops. Occasionally they make news by defending trees from bulldozers, but they rarely show up on talk shows, on the covers of magazines, on ballots, or on business pages. Instead, largely invisible except to one another, they go about learning the skills and mastering the tools necessary for meeting basic human needs. They grow food. They build shelters. They make clothes. They draw energy from sun and wind and wood. They get by with fewer possessions, and learn to repair the ones they have. They create much of their own entertainment, with homemade art, music, and stories. They derive pleasure from good work, human company, and the perennial show that nature puts on. So far as possible, they rear their children away from television and advertising. They buy as little as they can from the global economy, and instead they support local economies based on cooperation, barter, and sharing. They protect and restore woods, prairies, and swamps, making room for wildness.

I think of these people as builders of arks, for their ways and works are vessels designed to preserve from extinction not merely our fellow creatures, as on Noah's legendary ark, but also the wisdom necessary for dwelling in a place generation after generation without diminishing either the place or the planet. In their efforts to conserve skillful means and wild lands, they point the way beyond the rising flood to a new and durable civilization.

The flood I have in mind is partly the literal rise in sea level from global warming, but more generally it is the cumulative effect of our assault on Earth. Each year we manufacture and spew over the globe millions of tons of toxic chemicals. Some of these chemicals have thinned the ozone layer, exposing all organisms to higher doses of ultraviolet radiation. The smoke from our power plants and exhaust from our engines produce acid rain, which kills forests and freshwater lakes. By trawling the seas with mammoth ships, we have depleted most of the world's fisheries, some of them beyond the point of recovery. Pollution from rivers has created dead zones in the oceans, such as the one at the mouth of the Mississippi in the Gulf of Mexico. By irrigating crops, we have saturated millions of acres of land with salt, rendering it sterile. Through the use of heavy machinery in farming, we have lost much of our topsoil to erosion, and through the application of poisons we have reduced the fertility of the soil that remains. Through the clearing of forests, especially near the equator, we have enlarged the reach of deserts. By draining wetlands, paving fields, and moving plants and animals from continent to continent, we are driving to extinction countless other species, our impact rivaling the great cataclysm that snuffed out the dinosaurs some sixty-five million years ago.

Clearly, it's high time to build arks. Scientists have estimated that by the end of this century, if we carry on with current rates of habitat destruction, more than half of all the species now alive will have perished. This havoc is powered by the swelling number of human beings, multiplied by our increasing rates of consumption. For humankind to reach a population of a billion took hundreds of thousands of years, from the beginnings of our species to 1830. A second billion was added in just a hundred years, by 1930. A third billion was added in the next thirty years, a fourth in fifteen years, a fifth in eleven years. Our population is now approaching seven billion and growing by about ninety million per year, and some demographers expect it to reach between nine and eleven billion by the middle of this century. If you draw a graph of these numbers, you will produce what mathematicians call an exponential curve, one heading nearly straight up. Such growth cannot be sustained indefinitely, since it points toward infinity. Either by design or by disaster, the curve will peak, and human population will begin to decline. Already, the amount of fossil energy, fresh water, arable land, and food available per person is declining. As a consequence, the number of people suffering from malnutrition today is greater than the number of people alive a century ago.

So when I say that we are facing a worldwide flood, I am referring not only to the waves that will lap higher and higher on the shores of our continents as the icecaps melt, but also to the rising tide of human beings, the rising toll of chaos and misery, and the wholesale erasure of our fellow creatures.

The forest that the tree-sitters were trying to save is called Brown's Woods, after the local businessman who owned it. The owner, who is by all accounts a decent as well as a prosperous man, could have sold or even donated the woods to a land trust or the city of Bloomington, but he stood to make a tidy sum by selling it to the Indianapolis developer, so that is what he did. Landowners here and elsewhere make such decisions every day, usually without any public notice. Judging from remarks in the newspaper, Mr. Brown was clearly chagrined that such a fuss had been made about his sale of the woods for an apartment complex. No doubt he was sincere in declaring his relief that no one had been hurt during the arrests.

But of course people *have* been hurt, if you take into account the effects of losing those woods to concrete and brick, the increased traffic and pollution from the residents of the 208 new apartments, the greater crowding in parks and schools. The protesters hoped that moral and ecological arguments might prevail over economic ones. They spoke at meetings; they gave interviews to reporters; they held rallies. Out in Brown's Woods, they wove a web of yarn among the big trees, to symbolize the interrelationship of all life, and they laced the web with flowers. When the sheriff's crew showed up, however, the bulldozers tore through the yarn, crushed the flowers, brushed aside all the arguments. The heavy machinery was on loan from the Indianapolis developer. And a good thing, said the sheriff, because it would have cost his department a bundle to rent so much equipment. The developer could write off the cost as a business expense.

The arguments for turning Brown's Woods into the Canterbury House Apartments are familiar: people need somewhere to live; people need jobs; investors deserve a return on their capital; the city must grow. We can always think of reasons for subduing land to our desires.

Whatever the arguments, the upshot is that the felling of Brown's Woods has diminished our common wealth, and those who live here after us will inherit a grimmer, grimier place. We are not the only ones hurt. The hawks, the coyotes, the toads and salamanders, the spicebush butterflies and orb-weaver spiders will all have to leave, if they can outrun the bulldozers and chainsaws, and if they can find another refuge anywhere near the sprawling city. The red oaks and shagbark hickories have no such chance, nor do the dogwoods and dogtooth violets, the bloodroot and chanterelles. These neighbors have no say over the future of the neighborhood. They write no checks, cast no votes. They have no voice in how we use the land—unless some of us speak up for them, as the tree-sitters have tried to do.

You will recall that God sends the biblical flood in punishment for human corruption, sparing only the upright Noah, Noah's family, and a breeding pair of "every living thing" (Genesis 6:19; this and subsequent biblical quotations from the Revised Standard Version). God instructs Noah to build an ark and take refuge there along with a male and female of each species. Then come forty days and forty nights of rain. "And all flesh died that moved upon the earth, birds, cattle, beasts, all swarming creatures that swarm upon the earth, and every man; everything on the dry land in whose nostrils was the breath of life" (7:21–22). You might wonder why all the crows and crickets and other innocent breathers must drown for sins committed by humans, but the Bible does not say.

When the skies clear, Noah sends forth a raven and then a dove to search for dry land. The raven never returns; the dove comes back empty-billed on its first flight, returns bearing an olive leaf on the second flight, and after the third flight does not return at all. Reassured, Noah and his fellow passengers drift to shore and step onto solid earth. Pleased by Noah's obedience, God vows, "I will never again curse the ground because of man, for the imagination of man's heart is evil from his youth; neither will I ever again destroy every living creature as I have done. While the earth remains, seedtime and harvest, cold and heat, summer and winter, day and night, shall not cease" (8:21–22). It's a beautiful promise, one that softens considerably the image of the tyrant who sent the flood.

But the promise has a dark side, from which we are still suffering. For God says to Noah, "Be fruitful and multiply, and fill the earth. The fear of you and the dread of you shall be upon every beast of the earth, and upon every bird of the air, upon everything that creeps on the ground and all the fish of the sea; into your hand they are delivered. Every moving thing that lives shall be food for you; and as I gave you the green plants, I give you everything" (Genesis 9:1–3). The passage may be read as merely stating the plain truth: all beasts *do* live in dread of us, because we are clever enough to displace, capture, or kill every other species. Understood in this light, God's charge to Noah may be taken as a warning not to abuse our power. But the same words may also be read—and, in fact, have often been read—as justifying our utter dominion over nature. If every animal and plant was created to serve our needs, if everything has been given into our hands, then we may use the earth as we see fit. Read in this way, the passage becomes a license to loot the planet.

While such a reading might appeal to the most reckless of developers, it is firmly contradicted by the rest of Noah's story. A few verses later, we find a third variation on the promise, one that clearly limits our dominion. "Behold," God tells Noah, "I establish my covenant with you and your descendants after you, and with every living creature that is with you, the birds, the cattle, and every beast of the earth with you, as many as came out of the ark. I establish my covenant with you, that never again shall all flesh be cut off by the waters of a flood, and never again shall there be a flood to destroy the earth" (9:9–11). The God who speaks here sounds chastened, as if regretting the slaughter of so many innocent beings. This God is the creator and protector of crickets and crows, rattlesnakes and rotifers. This God cherishes *all* creatures, whether or not they go about on two legs, and by implication Noah is being told to cherish them as well.

The lesson we draw from the biblical flood depends on which of these rival traditions we embrace. One tradition blesses humans alone, conveying the whole of Earth to our use; the other blesses all creatures alike, granting to each species its own right to survive and flourish. The first view instructs us to fill the earth with our kind and to impose our will on all living things; the second instructs us to honor our fellow creatures, to show restraint in our uses of the earth, and to take our place modestly in the household of nature.

Those who wield the levers of power in our society generally hold by the first view. They insist on the sovereignty of human appetite. Nothing has value in their eyes except insofar as it can be bought or sold or otherwise used. They scorn the idea that animals or plants could have rights, even the right to survive. While they fight against the protection of existing species—mocking those who defend snail darters or spotted owls or redwoods—they support the engineering and patenting of new life forms, which can be turned more conveniently into cash. They resist every effort to preserve wilderness; they regard public land as an arena for private plunder; they reject any limits to growth; they seek to overthrow every barrier to drilling, mining, logging, road-building, polluting, or profit-making. By largely controlling the delivery of news, advertising, and entertainment, they tell us what to believe and what to buy, and they force-feed us a lethal vision of the good life.

Clearly, humans could not have survived without making use of the earth. Our ancestors hunted and fished, they gathered berries and seeds and roots, they fashioned clothing from skins and fibers, they cleared fields and planted grains, they domesticated animals, they cut down trees and dug up rocks and baked clay into bricks to build shelters, they harnessed fire and smelted ore into metal. The question is not whether we should use the earth, but to what degree and to what end. With only stone-tipped weapons, our ancestors drove many species of large animals to extinction; with hand tools, they felled enough trees to create deserts. Our need for prudence has grown along with the power of our technology, as stone points have given way to nuclear weapons, as bone hooks on fishing lines have given way to ocean-going trawlers pulling miles-long seines, as digging sticks have given way to draglines capable of stripping the tops from mountains in the search for coal. Likewise, as our population has grown from the few million people alive at the time Noah's story was written down to nearly seven billion today, so has our need for an ethic of restraint.

Noah's story offers us such an ethic in the call to protect *all* the creatures on the ark. Those who hear this call insist that human beings should be stewards rather than sovereign rulers. They insist that we belong to the community of soil, water, air, and all living things, and they seek to live in such a way as to preserve and enhance the health of this greater community. They accept limits to growth and limits to human population. Whether or not they've read the Bible, their actions are in keeping with God's command to Noah, which was to save not only those species that would be useful to human beings, but *everything*—the creepers and crawlers, the stingers and biters, the predators and parasites. From a religious perspective, these are all the handiwork of God, who loves Creation and wishes to preserve it. From an ecological perspective, each species is vital because it embodies an irreplaceable store of knowledge accumulated over millions of years, and it interacts with other species in ways far more intricate than we could ever fathom let alone recreate.

Religion and biology alike instruct us to honor all life. And so, recognizing that the earth has suffered great damage because of our carelessness, and realizing that many other species besides our own are in danger, those who believe in the solidarity of living things have set about building arks.

A book may be an ark, as *Walden* and *A Sand County Almanac* clearly are, ferrying an ethical vision through stormy times. Horse-logging, organic farming, solar designing, or other practices that protect the fertility and abundance of Earth may be arks. A co-op for sharing food or housing or tools might be an ark, and so might be a community chorus, an arts center, a backyard garden, a children's science museum, a yoga class, a school—any human structure, invention, or collaboration that preserves the wisdom necessary for meeting our needs without despoiling the planet.

Among the builders and tenders of arks, the ones who come closest to fulfilling Noah's task are the people who work at protecting and restoring wild lands. Some devote a portion or even the whole of their own land to providing habitat for other creatures. I know a man who is replanting a farmed-out piece of ground, acre by acre, to prairie; he measures the success of his work by the variety of birds and butterflies returning to his farm. I know farmers who are restoring a swamp by plugging up the drain tiles in a badly eroded cornfield. As the water pools once more, rushes and cattails rise around the margins, and beavers and raccoons and geese leave their footprints in the mud. With help from parents, children in our town have been planting trees and wildflowers on their school grounds, and city workers have begun restoring the riparian lushness and meandering flow of creeks in local parks. A group of Quakers bought property bordering a state forest just outside of our town, and they're turning it into a retreat center, where children can watch tadpoles or swing on grapevines, where adults can meditate and pray, where all can seek the spirit in nature.

Others save open space by forming land trusts, which acquire property outright through donation or purchase, or acquire conservation easements that protect land from development. The Nature Conservancy and the Trust for Public Land have been doing such work across the nation for decades, but now in addition there are local land trusts operating in all fifty states, more than sixteen hundred of them at present, and the number keeps growing. In my own home region of southern Indiana, the Sycamore Land Trust has combined gifts, grants, and federal and state conservation funds to protect a five-hundred-acre parcel of wet bottomland forest along Beanblossom Creek, which is home to a rookery for great blue herons. Every time I see one of these magisterial birds wading in a nearby lake or flying overhead with long legs trailing, I realize they might not be here at all without the Beanblossom Preserve.

Whether protected by government, trusts, or individuals, natural lands offer the last resort for other species as well as for those of our own species who crave contact with wildness. These preserves need not be large to be valuable; every scrap of ground can serve as an ark. Quite a few people in my city have dug up their lawns and planted their yards with native flowers, shrubs, and ferns. As one yard after another goes native, the roar and stink of mowers give way to the songs of birds and the smell of flowers. In summer, monarch butterflies on migration stop to collect nectar from blossoms, and in winter rabbits leave their tracks in the snow. All year, people walking by these exuberant yards pause on the sidewalks to gaze and listen, caught by a feral scent, a startling shape, a flash of life.

Yards with a bit of sun may also be planted in tomatoes, broccoli, and beans. My wife and I raise enough salad greens, garlic, and onions to share the abundance with our daughter and her husband, their two girls, and a few neighbors. Community gardens have sprung up on land provided by the city, complete with water spigot and compost bins. In the evenings and on weekends you can see families planting and weeding and harvesting, visiting with other gardeners, trading tips on cooking and canning. From early spring until late fall, a farmers' market brings into the heart of the city vegetables, fruits, honey, and flowers from local growers. You can buy sweet corn that was picked only hours before, and hand your money to a person who helped raise this bounty, and you can talk about how the soils and crops and kids are doing. Because you know the grower, you can also know that the food on your plate was neither sprayed with poisons nor injected with antibiotics; you know that it reached you from five or twenty miles away instead of five hundred or two thousand, and so it cost the earth far less in petroleum; and you know that you have circulated your money in the local economy.

Every unsprayed garden and unkempt yard, every meadow, marsh, and woods may become a reservoir for biological possibilities, keeping alive creatures who bear in their genes millions of years' worth of evolutionary discoveries. Every such refuge may also become a reservoir for spiritual possibilities, keeping alive our connection with the land, reminding us of our origins in the green world.

Ark-builders realize, however, that nothing is gained by creating refuges in one place, if we behave in a way that contributes to the despoiling of land somewhere else. If we're going to build arks, we should do everything we can to avoid swelling the flood. This means living more lightly. Since two-thirds of energy use in America goes for transportation, which also releases the bulk of our greenhouse gases, living lightly means, first of all, buying more fuel-efficient cars and driving them fewer miles; it means walking or bicycling whenever we can; it means flying less often and lobbying for passenger railway service. Since every item shipped to stores or to our front doors rides on petroleum, living lightly means buying as much as we can from local growers, makers, and merchants, instead of transnational corporations. It also means buying only what we need, avoiding fashions, learning to mend whatever we own and to make it last. It means seceding, so far as possible, from the global economy, which cares neither for the fate of the planet nor for the health of particular places.

The ark-builders understand the link between consumption and devastation: the more we consume—of gasoline, junk food, clothing, containers, electronic toys—the more the planet must be mined, bulldozed, clear-cut, and paved. Recognizing this, the ark-builders don't identify themselves as consumers but as conservers. Their aim in life is not to devour as much stuff as possible, but to savor the necessities of life. They learn to provide for themselves as many of those necessities as they can, from growing food to rewiring an old house, from playing the banjo to sewing quilts. They share tools, cars, and recipes with friends and neighbors. They exchange labor with others in their community, trading a load of firewood for a tune-up, say, or swapping a haircut for a massage. The ark-builders don't rush from one sensation to the next, as the media propose, but instead they relish the pleasures of an unhurried pace. They hang their laundry outdoors, enjoying the sunshine, instead of stuffing it in a machine. They cook their own food instead of grabbing a sack of sugar and fat in a drive-through lane. They take walks or sit for talks with people they love, instead of buying a ticket to the latest craze. They meet the world in the flesh, instead of through a screen. They remember how to dream and laugh without benefit of electricity.

None of this would have seemed strange to our grandparents. Thrift is normal; it's what sensible people have always practiced, in every land. What's abnormal is the binge of consumption that the rich nations have been on for the past few decades. The ark-builders know this binge will pass, and the sooner the better. Meanwhile, they do what they can to hold back the flood of devastation.

By protecting wild land, they are helping to preserve the biological heritage—the seed stock, the diversity of species, the intricate web of fertility—that we will need to replenish the earth after the flood recedes. By living simply, by meeting more and more of their own needs from local and renewable sources, they are conserving the skills, knowledge, and values that our descendants will need in order to live decent lives without impoverishing the planet. By forming alternative communities, they are creating islands of sanity and integrity from which a new civilization may spread.

When the tree-sitters were arrested in Brown's Woods, the sheriff was quoted in the newspaper as saying, "We want to do this slow and easy, so no one gets injured—so everybody has their say and can get on with their lives." What he didn't seem to grasp was that the protesters *were* getting on with their lives. They were expressing their love for a piece of Earth. In this dispute over Brown's Woods, one side has its say by sending in police and bulldozers, and by throwing the protesters in jail; the other side has its say by weaving yarn among the trees and speaking plain words on behalf of the greater community of all beings.

When the "Bluebird 16," as they came to be known, were arraigned on charges of criminal trespass, they all requested jury trials. "They want to clog up the system," the county prosecutor complained. "They just want to make this as public and drawn out as possible." Of course the protesters want to make the dispute public. That's in the nature of civil disobedience, and in the nature of any democratic challenge to legal but harmful behavior. One of the defendants said that the goal is to put sprawl itself on trial, along with the developers, investors, and officials who send bulldozers into every open space.

of sanctuaries, blooming across our cities and countryside, will not be spacious enough if the rest of the planet becomes an industrial wasteland.

Ultimately, there will be no security for life on Earth unless we see the whole planet as an ark. We are not the captains of this vessel, although we may flatter ourselves by thinking so. We are common passengers, and yet because we are both clever and numerous, we bear a unique responsibility to do everything we can to assure that this one precious ark will stay afloat, with all the least and greatest of our fellow travelers safely on board.

Common Wealth

*W*hat is being sold to us as the "American way of life" is mostly a cheat and a lie. It is an infantile dream of endless consumption, endless novelty, and endless play. It is bad for us and bad for the earth.

We need a dream worthy of grown-ups, one that values simplicity over novelty, conservation over consumption, harmony over competition, community over ego. We need a story that celebrates the true source of our wellbeing, not in the private wealth we hold as individuals or as corporations but in the common wealth we share as members of the human family. We need a new vision of the good life. Or, rather, we need to recover and refresh an old vision, one well known to our ancestors but now largely forgotten.

In England, "the commons" originally referred to lands and waters that were used by the community as a whole—the pastures, woodlots, tillable fields, springs, lakes, and rivers on which everyone depended for sustenance. Even if the land was owned by a feudal lord, a church, or a monarch, it was partly or entirely open to use by those who lived nearby, and the terms of that use were defined primarily by the community rather than by the owner.

If one goes back far enough in time, of course, the whole earth was a commons—as the Americas were at the time Europeans first encountered the indigenous people they called "Indians." One must be wary of making generalizations about the hundreds of cultures that evolved in the Western Hemisphere before 1500, but everything I have read suggests that, while native tribes recognized territories for hunting and gathering, they did not recognize private ownership of portions of the earth.

The Europeans who colonized the Americas began carving up this commons and turning it into private property, as the wealthy classes were busily doing back in England and on the Continent. Between the 1500s and the mid-1800s, nearly all of the English commons were privatized, initially through the actions of landlords and later through acts of Parliament. In the process, centuries-old relationships between people and place were torn apart; a view of land as the source of live-lihood for the whole community was replaced by a view of land as a commodity to be bought and sold for the benefit of the propertied class. Those who did not own land became, if they were lucky, the tenants or wage servants of those who did; and if they were unlucky, they starved.

Where there had once been free passage for people and animals, now hedges, fences, wardens, and legal barriers blocked the way. The legal barriers were imposed by Parliament in bills called "acts of enclo-sure," and "enclosure" thus became the shorthand term for privatizing the commons. The first great surge of enclosures occurred in the late Middle Ages, propelled by the lucrative wool trade. By 1516, the lead-ing character in Sir Thomas More's *Utopia* could lament that mild-mannered sheep, grazing on what had once been common land, were devouring men and villages as well as grass.

We should not idealize the medieval commons. While peasants were assured of access to most of the sources of subsistence, they were also bound by feudal relations to the local lord—to give him a portion of their crops, for example, or to work a certain number of days each year in his fields, or to take up arms in his militia. We are well rid of feudalism. What we need to recover is the older culture of the com-mons on which feudalism was imposed and which feudalism eventu-ally destroyed, a culture that emphasized the equitable sharing of the elements needed for survival. Protecting the resources on which our wellbeing depends is a matter of prudence; making sure they are avail-able to all, and not merely to the rich, is a matter of justice.

By the middle of the eighteenth century, Jean-Jacques Rousseau could trace the origins of social inequality to the privatizing of the commons:

> The first man who, having enclosed a piece of land, thought of saying, "This is mine" and found people simple enough to believe him, was the true founder of civil society. How many crimes, wars, murders; how

much misery and horror the human race would have been spared if someone had pulled up the stakes and filled in the ditch and cried out to his fellow men: "Beware of listening to this impostor. You are lost if you forget that the fruits of the earth belong to everyone and that the earth itself belongs to no one!"

In a gloss on this passage, Voltaire remarked, "Behold the philosophy of a beggar who would like the rich to be robbed by the poor!"

The following centuries have shown that Voltaire needn't have worried. By the end of the nineteenth century, 99 percent of England's agricultural land was owned by just over half a percent of the population. Except for occasional setbacks, as during the French Terror and the Bolshevik Revolution, the rich in Europe and the United States have easily held their own, and they have done so, in large part, by enclosing more and more of the commons. Today, the fences encircle far more than land. In America, individuals and corporations are patenting life forms and genetic information; they are profiting from scientific research conducted at public expense; they are selling water drawn from aquifers and springs, and they are exploiting public reservoirs for farming and real estate development in arid regions; they are building in flood-prone areas thanks to flood insurance underwritten by taxpayers; they are hijacking the public airwaves and the internet; they are drilling for oil, mining for minerals, felling timber, and grazing livestock on public lands, paying fees far below market values or paying nothing at all; they are polluting the air, water, and soils and passing on the cost of that pollution to all of us. These private grabs of public goods are widening the gulf not only between rich and poor individuals but also between rich and poor nations, even as they are degrading the commons.

Enclosures are by no means the only threat to the health of the biosphere. Anyone who takes an honest look at the evidence realizes that natural systems are breaking down under the pressure of a swelling human population, which consumes more resources, releases more toxins, disrupts more habitat, and drives more species to extinction year by year. The consequent human suffering—from war, drought, famine, and disease—is incalculable and unconscionable. As a result of these disasters, we now realize that we depend on far more than the lands and waters originally belonging to the commons, although of course lands and waters are crucial. We depend on countless shared goods, from a stable climate and a prolific ocean to honest government and excellent schools.

We could speak about the whole realm of shared goods as *the commons,* as Vandana Shiva does in talking about the indigenous knowledge bound up in the strains of rice and wheat developed by generations of Indian farmers; as Jeremy Rifkin does in warning against efforts to privatize the human genome; as Peter Barnes does in proposing how to defend the atmosphere from pollution; as David Bollier does in protesting the giveaway of knowledge derived from publicly funded research; or as Elinor Ostrom does in writing about the protection of ocean fisheries.

While *the commons* is a perfectly serviceable term with a noble history, the one I prefer to use is *common wealth,* which originally meant *the general welfare.* We need to seize every opportunity of speaking more vigorously on behalf of the general welfare, especially in the United States, where public discourse has been taken over almost entirely by the rhetoric of individualism and free enterprise. I separate the compound word into its two parts, *common* and *wealth,* to distinguish my usage from that of Thomas Hobbes, John Locke, and other political philosophers, who equated the *commonwealth*—one word—with the body politic.

As I understand it, the common wealth embraces much more than the body politic; it embraces all those natural and cultural goods that we share by virtue of our membership in the human family. A short list of these goods would include the air, waters, soils, and oceans; outer space; the electromagnetic spectrum; the human gene pool and the diversity of species; language in all its forms, including mathematics and music; knowledge in all its forms, from art to zoology; all manner of artifacts and machines, from stone scrapers to supercomputers; the practical arts such as cooking, building, herding, and farming; the practice of medicine; the body of law, the structures of democratic government, and the traditions of civil liberty; parks, community gardens, state and national forests, wildlife refuges, and protected wilderness areas; museums, libraries, schools, plazas, and other public spaces.

None of us, as individuals or even as nations, could create these goods from scratch, or replace them if they were lost. For example, no amount of ingenuity or effort on our part could restore balance to a destabilized global climate, mend the tattered ozone layer, or revive an ocean fishery that has been depleted below the threshold required for biological recovery. And none of us creates wealth purely through our own efforts, but only by drawing on this vast inheritance. At most, we may add some mite of value—an idea, an invention, a song—but whatever we contribute is minuscule compared to the riches we inherit. We are born into the legacy of the common wealth, and we pass it on, either enhanced or diminished, to future generations.

For the past quarter century, American politics has been dominated by attempts to ransack the commons for the benefit of the few. This plundering takes many forms: below-cost timber sales in national forests, over-grazing of public lands by privately owned livestock, licensing of the airwaves to media monopolies, patenting of organisms, oil drilling in wildlife refuges, subsidies for the nuclear industry and agribusiness, pork barrel highway projects, sweetheart deals for military contractors, off-shore tax havens for corporations, waiver of clean air regulations for power plants and of clean-water regulations for livestock operations, the opening of national parks to snowmobiles, on and on. Legislatures and agencies charged with protecting the public domain have colluded with corporations and individuals to give it away or to sell it off at bargain-basement prices. The net result of all this plundering is to diminish the wealth we hold in common.

Our politicians and merchants rarely seem to notice that we hold any wealth in common. The story they tell is almost entirely about private wealth and private solutions. If the streets are unsafe, instead of reducing the poverty that causes crime, buy an alarm system, move into a gated community, pack a gun. If the public schools are failing, instead of fixing them, put your kids in private schools. If the water is tainted, don't work to clean it up; buy your own supply in bottles. If the roads are clogged, don't push for public transportation; buy a bigger car. If cancer is epidemic, instead of addressing the causes, try the latest therapies. If the future of Social Security looks insecure, instead of overhauling the system, funnel the dollars into private accounts, so those who guess right on the market will win and those who guess wrong will lose. If nearly fifty million Americans lack any form of health insurance and tens of millions more lack adequate coverage, instead of expanding Medicare to cover everyone fairly, establish private health accounts so the rich can buy superior care and the middle class can take their chances and the poor can live in fear of accident or illness. Even many churches, which might challenge this epidemic of selfishness, enlarge their congregations by preaching the gospel of prosperity rather than material simplicity, and personal salvation rather than service to one's neighbor.

I focus on the United States because it is the society I know best and because, through its military and economic power, it has a disproportionate influence on the fate of the earth. At less than 5 percent of the world's population, Americans account for 25 percent of the world's annual consumption of oil and other non-renewable natural resources. American films, television programs, and advertising shape the appetites of citizens everywhere. The dominant media in our society proclaim that happiness, meaning, and security are to be found through piling up money and buying things. Whatever troubles us, shopping can fix it; whatever hollowness we feel, shopping can fill it; whatever questions haunt us, shopping can provide the answers. A recent billboard for a brand of cigarettes used the slogan, "Get More Stuff," and that might serve as the motto for our entire commercial culture. Another billboard shows a commuter chugging a bottle of dairy drink while dashing to catch a train, above the slogan: GRAB. GULP. GO. Joined together, those two slogans—"Get more stuff. Grab, gulp, go!"—could be the mantra for our hectic, profligate civilization.

Our political culture delivers pretty much the same message— which isn't surprising, since the corporations that flood the media with their ads also fund political campaigns and dictate legislation. After the attacks of September 11, 2001, when Americans longed to know how we could help our country, politicians told us to haul out our charge cards and run up some debt. When millions of Americans wondered how we could reduce our dependence on oil, and thus our entanglement with despotic regimes in the Middle East, our leaders told us to get in our cars and drive, or climb into airplanes and fly. When Americans look around at this richest of nations and see public debt piling up, hospitals closing, schools failing, forests dying, prison populations swelling, farmland and wetlands disappearing under subdivisions and malls, children going without medical care, and homeless people sleeping on the streets, our leaders offer us a tax cut, so we'll have more money in our pockets. And 40 percent of the benefits from those tax cuts go to the wealthiest 1 percent of Americans, who already have more money in their pockets than they know what to do with.

A week before the first anniversary of the September 11th attacks, a two-page ad in the *New York Times* for a cell phone service used the slogan, "Get More," and then listed two dozen things you would get more of by purchasing this product, including more laughs, more party invites, and more second glances; with this phone you'd also get more friendly, available, motivated, and involved; you'd get more time with your kids, more of what you want, "more and more and more." Those claims are almost entirely false, of course, and we could laugh them off if they weren't beamed at us, on behalf of one product or another, through every channel of communication, twenty-four hours a day.

The common wealth is being devoured by the so-called free market, where everything is for sale, and nothing is shared. The pursuit of profit clearly has a role to play in any economy, yet in our own time, and especially in the United States, it threatens to swallow everything from the national forests to the electromagnetic spectrum. In order to restore balance and to defend the sources of wellbeing, we need a countervailing vision that is at least as powerful as that of the unfettered marketplace.

I'm guessing that everyone reading these lines has at least glimpsed such a redemptive vision. You've dreamed of living in a household and a neighborhood suffused with love and respect. You've dreamed of living in a community that is just, beautiful, harmonious, and durable, a community that values all its citizens, that makes room for other species, that draws energy from wind and sun, that meets many of its own needs from local sources, that nourishes learning and the arts, and that protects these blessings for future generations. You've dreamed of belonging to a nation of such communities, and to a world of such nations.

The work of creating wise and loving communities begins with cherishing our common wealth. I speak of it as *common* because it is ordinary and because it is shared. The word derives from a verb meaning to exchange or barter; it suggests a giving and receiving. The etymology of *wealth* leads back to *weal* and *well*; to be wealthy means, at root, to be well, to flourish. So *common wealth* embraces all those shared conditions and gifts necessary for human flourishing. It is not an inventory of property or inert resources; it is a living, sustaining web of energies, creatures, ideas, and activities. You won't see these treasures for sale in the mall. You won't see them advertised on TV. You won't discover them in corporate balance sheets or the gross domestic product. You'll rarely hear them spoken of with pride by politicians, who seem hell-bent on auctioning off everything that might have the word *public* attached to it.

Where you're likely to hear people talking about our common wealth is at a block party, a union meeting, a street festival, or a concert in the park. You're likely to hear such talk among people cleaning up a river, planting trees on a ravaged hillside, reclaiming an abandoned rail yard for a playground, turning a trash-filled lot into a community garden. In short, you'll hear testimony to our shared wealth wherever people come together to preserve, restore, or create something for the good of the community, and not merely for their own private advantage.

In the raw young American democracy, Alexis de Tocqueville observed an uneasy balance between the pursuit of personal advantage and a concern for the common good. On the one hand, he lamented an obsession with money-making and private gain, a selfishness that amounted at times to solipsism: "not only does democracy make every man forget his ancestors, but it hides his descendants and separates his contemporaries from him; it throws him back forever upon himself alone, and threatens in the end to confine him entirely within the solitude of his own heart." On the other hand, he remarked, "In no country in the world, do the citizens make such exertions for the common weal. I know of no people who have established schools so numerous and efficacious, places of public worship better suited to the wants of the inhabitants, or roads kept in better repair."

Since Tocqueville made those observations in the 1830s, the balance between solipsism and altruism, if such a balance ever existed, has certainly been lost. The spirit of cooperation and philanthropy that so bedazzled the visiting Frenchman is still alive in America, but it has been overshadowed by rampant privatism. The myth of the social compact, which emphasizes our dependence on one another, has been largely displaced by the myth of self-reliance.

In the essay that more than any other piece of writing gave currency to the term "self-reliance," Ralph Waldo Emerson insisted, "do not tell me, as a good man did to-day, of my obligation to put all poor men in good situations. Are they *my* poor? I tell thee, thou foolish philanthropist, that I grudge the dollar, the dime, the cent I give to such men as do not belong to me and to whom I do not belong." Delivered first as a public lecture and then printed in 1841, "Self-Reliance" was a bold, and, at the time, perhaps a necessary challenge to the pressure for conformity in ethical and religious matters. Tocqueville noted this pressure in one of his characteristically ambivalent observations about the fledgling democracy: "In the principle of equality I very clearly discern two tendencies; the one leading the mind of every man to untried thoughts, the other which would prohibit him from thinking at all." Just over a decade after publication of "Self-Reliance," Henry David Thoreau echoed Emerson's sentiments in *Walden:* "While my townsmen and women are devoted in so many ways to the good of their fellows, I trust that one at least may be spared to other and less humane pursuits. You must have a genius for charity as well as for anything else. As for Doing-good, that is one of the professions which are full."

It is crucial to remember that for Emerson, the small "self" of the individual was to be guided by the transcendent Self in which "all things find their common origin." His call for "self-reliance" arose from the firm belief that each of us has direct access, through the soul, to "the aboriginal Self, on which a universal reliance may be grounded." Moreover, he insisted, "The relations of the soul to the divine spirit are so pure that it is profane to seek to interpose helps." That belief has its own dangers, as every religious zealot proves. But if we reject all claims for such a transcendent Self, then each of us is locked into the small self, which is not dependably generous or loving or wise. If the only guide we acknowledge is the ego, then we and our neighbors are in trouble.

Stripped of its religious constraints, the rhetoric of self-reliance that Emerson and Thoreau used to defend the autonomy of individual conscience has gradually devolved, over the past century and a half, into a naked defense of selfishness. In a letter published in my hometown newspaper this past winter, a man complained about the law requiring him to shovel his sidewalk after a snow; he pointed out that he never used the sidewalk, and so the shoveling only benefited other people, and helping other people, he concluded, was socialism.

On a trip not long ago I flew on an airline whose slogan is "One World Revolves Around You"; I stayed overnight in a motel whose slogan is "It's All About You"; I saw military recruiting posters enticing volunteers into "An Army of One"; I noticed a billboard featuring a young woman in a strapless green dress, holding a red spike-heel shoe in one hand, resting her chin in the other hand, her eyes and lacquered lips expressing a combination of boredom and disdain, and below her picture the caption: "I am what I shop."

Nearly all advertising delivers the same message: you, the isolated consumer, are the center of the universe; your pleasure, comfort, status, looks, convenience, and distraction are all that matter; you will find happiness and fulfillment through buying this product or service; the entire Earth is a warehouse of raw materials at your service. By the age of 21 the average American has encountered over thirty million ads, in one medium or another. That typical young American has also spent more hours watching television than attending school. For all practical purposes, television *is* school, and saturation advertising is the voice of the ravenous ego forever whispering in our ears.

The political assault on the common wealth and the commercial appeal to "consumers" go hand-in-hand. Both urge us to grab whatever we can, to indulge our appetites without regard for the needs of community, without gratitude to the people whose labor supports us, without concern for future generations, without acknowledging that we share the earth with millions of other species or that we draw every drop of our sustenance from nature. While the world decays around us, we are urged to buy our way to security, as if we could withdraw inside a cocoon of money. This story, the dominant one in America today, is a self-centered fantasy that leads to loneliness for the individual and disaster for the world.

We need an alternative story, one that appeals to our generosity and compassion rather than our selfishness. We need a story that measures wealth not by the amount of money held in private hands nor by the stock market index but by the condition of the commons. We need a story that links the health of individuals to the health of communities, a story that reminds us we inhabit not merely a house or a city or a nation but a planet. Rather than defining us as consumers, this new story would define us as conservers; rather than cultivating narcissism, it would inspire neighborliness; rather than exhorting us to chase after fashions, it would invite us to find joy in everyday blessings—in the voice of a child or a bird, in music and books, in gardening and strolling, in sharing food and talk. To live by such a story, we need not be sages or saints; we need simply be awake to the real sources of the good life.

In crafting such a story, we might begin by reimagining where we live. Most of us, when asked for our address, will give a street number, a postal code, or other markers of place, but we are unlikely to name the nearest river. As one step toward reviving a concern for the common wealth, we could inscribe on the covers of our phonebooks a map of the local watershed. Grown-ups would be puzzled at first by this way of describing their true address, but I expect that children would readily grasp what it means. In elementary schools across the country, with help from teachers and parents, students are mapping their watersheds and monitoring the quality of rivers and lakes. In some communities, after identifying sources of pollution, children have offered testimony to city councils and environmental protection boards. Youngsters readily understand that rivers and lakes gather whatever falls or is dumped on the land, and that streams reveal the state of health for the whole watershed. They understand that each of us lives in the embrace of a river.

My own home in southern Indiana is embraced by the east and west forks of the White River, a name that has always struck me as utterly bland. I would have much preferred the Delaware name, *Wah-pi-ha-ni*, which sounds more evocative and musical to my ears. However, when I asked a Shawnee friend for a translation of *Wah-pi-ha-ni*, he put on a solemn look, leaned close to my ear, and confided, "It means White River." So I have resigned myself to the English name.

With a watershed of 11,350 square miles, wholly contained within Indiana, the White drains roughly a third of the state. So the quality of its water is a fair measure of how well government, municipalities, businesses, farmers, and ordinary citizens of Indiana are caring for this precious common resource. The verdict is: not very well. The White ranks high on lists of the nation's threatened rivers—not because of depletion, as in rivers of the arid southwest, or because of dams, as in rivers of the mountainous northwest, but because of pollution. In the upper and lower reaches, it collects runoff from glacial plains, where the deep topsoil is devoted mainly to soybeans and corn and is liberally sprayed with pesticides and herbicides; throughout the watershed, including the unglaciated southern hills where I live, it gathers runoff from lawns, parking lots, highways, factory outlet pipes, municipal dumps, and overburdened sewer systems. The resulting stew of toxins has made it dangerous to drink straight from the river, swim in the river, or eat fish drawn from the river. A few years ago, five million fish were killed by a single factory discharge. The Indiana Department of Environmental Management duly issues warnings. But the word *management* is a misnomer here; no one is managing the White River. At best, our state and federal agencies are monitoring its decline.

I spoke recently with a man whose job is to travel around our watershed explaining to farmers new regulations that limit, for the first time ever, the amounts and kinds of poisons they can spray on their land. His standard reception is to be called a communist. The Indiana Farm Bureau as well as the agrichemical companies declare that it is un-American to restrict what a man can do on his own land or what a corporation can sell. Likewise, many developers, industrialists, loggers, and homeowners resist any constraints that might cost them money or sweat. In doing what is cheapest, easiest, and most profitable for themselves, they are obeying the rational self-interest so famously celebrated by Adam Smith and so assiduously defended by advocates of the free market. Added together, however, these selfish choices do not magically serve the "public good," as if guided by an "invisible hand," as Smith predicted, but instead they defile a public good called the White River.

Under the twin banners of property rights and free enterprise, rivers are being spoiled all across America. Elsewhere, the abuse may come from mine tailings, power plants, livestock feedlots, or paper mills; from barge traffic or jet skis; from the pumping of vast quantities of water for resorts in the desert; or from mountain-top removal for coal mining. The pace of such abuse has increased along with growth in population, in the power of technology, and in the sway of corporations. Regulation alone will not be enough to reverse the trend. In spite of treaties, there are constant battles over allocation of water from the Colorado, for example, and the river is so overdrawn that scarcely any flow reaches the sea. The Clean Water Act has led to gradual improvement in some rivers, but in many cases, it is cheaper for a company to pay fines for poisoning a river than to clean up its effluents. No matter what rules are on the books, any given administration in Washington can choose to reinterpret the law, weaken it, or ignore it entirely.

Of course we need wise legislation at the local, state, and national level to protect our rivers, along with the rest of our common wealth. But what we need even more is a change in mindset. Here again, we can begin by reviving an old mindset, one that has been enshrined in cultural practices and legal principles for centuries. To stay with rivers for a moment longer, I could cite as illustration the edict issued by the Roman Emperor Justinian in 535 CE:

> By the law of nature these things are common to mankind—the air, running water, the sea, and consequently the shores of the sea.... All rivers and ports are public; hence the right of fishing in a port, or in rivers, is common to all men.... The public use of the banks of a river is part of the law of nations, just as is that of the river itself.

In 1225, King John of England was forced to accept the Magna Carta, which prohibited him from offering to individuals exclusive use of rivers or any other portion of the commons. These protections came to be embodied in English common law as the Public Trust Doctrine, according to which the monarch, and later the state, acts as steward of the lands and waters for the benefit of all the people and of future generations. Similar legal doctrines evolved in France and Spain, and they were ferried across the Atlantic as the European powers established colonies in the New World.

A method for efficiently and fairly distributing water in arid country, introduced into Spain during the Muslim occupation, came to be called *acequia,* a word transliterated from Arabic meaning *irrigation ditch.* The Semitic root is a verb that means *to give to drink.* In the word and in the practice, there is an implicit ethical principle: since water is necessary for survival, equitable access to fresh water should be available to all human beings who share a place. No person, no corporation, should claim a monopoly on water. The acequia system was carried over to the Spanish territories in the American Southwest, where it was no doubt influenced by the irrigation practices of the Pueblo, and where it set a pattern for communal water-sharing that lasted for centuries. Even more important than the ditches that gave the acequia system its name were the rules governing the allocation of water, rules embodying the ancient belief that water is a common good, to be protected for the benefit of the entire community.

Although there has been relentless pressure to privatize water, especially in the arid west, until recently U.S. courts have generally upheld the view of rivers as a public resource to be shared by all. For example, in a 1950 opinion the Supreme Court stated:

> As long ago as the institutes of Justinian running waters, like the air and the sea, were *res communes*—things common to all and property of none. Such was the doctrine spread by the civil-law commentators and embodied in the Napoleonic Code and in Spanish law. This concept passed into common law.

It is hard to imagine today's Supreme Court issuing such an opinion. Venerable though they may be, legal principles such as the Public Trust Doctrine and cultural practices such as the acequia system are losing their force as our courts are increasingly filled by jurists for whom private property rights trump communal property rights. Any doctrine or practice that interferes with an individual's or a corporation's power to make money is more and more likely to be struck down, if not by U.S. courts then by international tribunals established by the World Trade Organization, the North American Free Trade Agreement, the General Agreement on Tariffs and Trade, or some other of the global instruments aimed at making the world safe for commerce.

As I said earlier, much as we need wise laws and socially responsible courts, they alone will not protect our rivers or the rest of our public goods. The only sure protection is a citizenry that clearly recognizes and fiercely defends the common wealth as the prime source of our wellbeing, and as our legacy to future generations.

Fortunately, many people sense this need. Across our country and around the world, people are shaping a new story about the sources of peace and plenty. You can see the story come alive in farmers' markets, housing co-ops, land trusts, neighborhood councils, and town theaters. You can see it in free medical clinics and Habitat for Humanity building sites. You can see it in the Green Belt Movement, which began in Kenya and which is now spreading trees and democracy across Africa. You can witness the story unfolding in citizen forums and simple living collectives, in shelters for abused women and children, in efforts to restore eagles and wolves. You can hear the hum of it in watershed councils formed to clean up rivers.

Those who embrace this new story are recovering wisdom that was well known to our ancestors. Writing soon after the American Revolution, Benjamin Franklin gave voice to an altruistic impulse that inspired many of our nation's founders when he explained why he had chosen not to patent his invention of a more efficient woodstove: "That, as we enjoy great advantages from the inventions of others, we should be glad to serve others by any invention of ours; and this we should do freely and generously." This attitude may sound quaint in our time, when individuals and corporations seek to patent or copyright everything on Earth, from the human genome to campfire songs. Yet only half a century ago, Jonas Salk refused to claim a patent on the polio vaccine, and today, this regard for the common good is showing up in new initiatives, such as the development of open-source software or the creation of a free digital library on the internet.

When the American experiment was still young, and still infused with revolutionary idealism, Tocqueville found citizens eager to serve the common wealth:

Thus, the most democratic country on the face of the earth is that in which men have, in our time, carried to the highest perfection the art of pursuing in common the object of their common desires, and have applied this new science to the greatest number of purposes. Is this the result of accident? or is there in reality any necessary connection between the principle of association and that of equality?

We know now that there is indeed a connection between the principle of equality and the practice of cooperation. In a true democracy, citizens do not look to an aristocracy, an oligarchy, a church, a corporation, or a distant government to meet the needs of the community; we roll up our sleeves, join with our neighbors, and set to work. In spite of what the media tell us, we know that the good life is not for sale. We understand that the good life is something we make together, in partnership with other people and in harmony with nature. We realize that happiness, health, security, and meaning come to us primarily through our membership in the common wealth, which we must therefore strive to preserve and enrich.

Love of our common wealth is a root impulse behind countless acts of gratitude and kindness that ordinary people perform every day. We all feel it, but we don't always know how to speak of it, or we speak of it so quietly that our story is drowned out by the blare of consumerism. We need to speak up, to say boldly why we fight for a just economy, inspiring schools, decent housing, and universal health care; why we protect open space, why we clean up rivers and replant forests; why we look after the ailing and the elderly; why we insist that government be a force for public good. In a society obsessed with competition, we need to say why we practice cooperation. In a culture addicted to instant gratification, we need to champion long-term healing.

The glorification of private wealth will go on around the clock, in every medium, without any help from us. We need to counter that chorus by lifting our voices in praise of the wealth we share, recalling how our lives depend on one another, on generations past and future, on the bountiful Earth and all its creatures, on the spirit that lifts us into being and sustains us through every moment and reclaims us in the end.

A Few Earthy Words

It might be said that all much-used,
debased words are looking for restoration,
for revivifying contexts.

—STEPHEN DUNN

*I*n a speech delivered in 1952, Rachel Carson warned: "Mankind has gone very far into an artificial world of his own creation. He has sought to insulate himself, in his cities of steel and concrete, from the realities of earth and water and the growing seed. Intoxicated with a sense of his own power, he seems to be going farther and farther into more experiments for the destruction of himself and his world."

Carson voiced these worries before the triumph of television or shopping malls, before the advent of air-conditioning, personal computers, video games, the internet, cell phones, cloning, genetic engineering, and a slew of other inventions that have made the artificial world ever more seductive. Unlike the natural world, the artificial world is made for us. It feeds our bellies and minds with tasty pabulum; it shelters us from discomfort and sickness; it proclaims our ingenuity; it flatters our pride. Snug inside bubbles fashioned from concrete and steel, from silicon and plastic and words, we can pretend we are running the planet.

By contrast, the natural world was not made for our comfort or convenience. It preceded us by billions of years, and it will outlast us; it mocks our pride, because it surpasses our understanding and control; it can be dangerous and demanding; while it nourishes and inspires us, it will eventually reclaim our bodies. We should not be surprised that increasing numbers of people choose to live entirely indoors, leaving buildings only to ride in airplanes or cars, viewing the great outside, if they view it at all, through sealed windows, but more often gazing into screens, listening to human chatter, cut off from "the realities of earth and water and the growing seed."

The more time we spend inside human constructions, the more likely we are to forget that these bubbles float in the great ocean of nature. A decade before Carson issued her warning, Aldo Leopold in *A Sand County Almanac* recognized this danger as the central challenge facing the conservation movement: How do we nurture a land ethic in people who have less and less contact with land? How do we inspire people to take care of their home places if they feel no sense of place?

If we aim to foster a culture of conservation, we'll have to work at changing a host of things, from ads to zoos, from how we put food on our plates to how we imagine our role in the universe. Out of all these necessary changes, I wish to speak about one that is close to my heart as a storyteller, which is the need to root language once more in the earth. We need to recover the fertile meanings of words that arise out of our long evolutionary contact with dirt and wind, rivers and woods, animals and plants.

Down at the roots of language, we often find an earthy wisdom. Take the word *growth,* for example. When Donella Meadows and her colleagues published a report in 1972 on the prospects for the continued expansion of the human economy, they called their book *The Limits to Growth.* The very title provoked outrage in many circles, because a prime article in the techno-industrial creed is that there *are* no limits to growth. According to this creed, any constraints imposed by nature will be overcome by technical ingenuity or the free market. Mining, drilling, pumping, clearing, manufacturing, and consuming—along with the human population that drives it all—will expand forever, the boosters claim. Politicians and business leaders speak of growth as unbounded and unambiguously good.

Our ancestors knew better. If we dig down to the root of *growth,* we find a verb that means to turn green, as grass does in the spring. In fact, *grow, grass,* and *green* all rise from the same Indo-European stem. Grass turns green in the spring, shoots up vigorously during the summer, then dies back and lies fallow through the winter. Season after season, the wilted grass turns to humus, enriching the soil. Molded into this word, therefore, is a recognition that growth is bounded, that it obeys the cycles of sun and rain, that it generates more fertility than it uses up.

If the phrase *sustainable growth* means perpetual expansion, then it is a delusion. Cancer shows that rampant growth soon becomes malignant. The sprawl of cities over the countryside and the spread of bellies over belts teach us that, beyond a certain point, expansion leads to misery, if not disaster. Nothing in nature expands forever. Certainly nothing on Earth grows unchecked, neither bodies nor cities nor economies. Buried in the word *growth* is the wisdom of people blessed with outdoor understanding, people who watched the grass rise and fall each year like a green wave.

The word *resource* embodies a similar insight. As we commonly use the word, it means "raw material," something we burn for energy, pulp for paper, or mine for steel. We speak of natural resources, human resources, financial resources, in each case referring to one kind of stuff that can be used to make other kinds of stuff. But the root meaning of *resource* is to spring up again. *Source* and *surge* both derive from a verb meaning to rise. A *re*-source is something that rises anew, like grass in a meadow or water in a spring.

In the world of hunters, gatherers, herders, and planters, what bounty surges forth time and again, year in and year out? The light and warmth of sun, the life-giving water of rain and snow, the ebb and flow of tides; alewives and salmon returning to spawn; migrating bison and caribou; trees for canoes and shelters and fires; berries and seeds; fruits and nuts; corn and beans and squash; lambs, calves, children, and chicks. In traditional cultures, all these blessings were surrounded by ceremonies of respect, for people who lived on the bounty of nature understood the need to protect the source.

In light of this wisdom, fish in the sea are only a resource so long as their breeding grounds are preserved and their numbers are not decimated. Clean air and water renew themselves only so long as we do not fill them with poisons. Topsoil is a resource only so long as we do not sterilize it with chemicals or squander it to erosion. Coal, oil, iron ore, and the other materials we drill for or mine are not resources at all, because they cannot be replenished. Nor is money a resource, because it brings nothing into the world, it merely divvies up what's already here. The wild abundance of the planet is quickly being exhausted because we have seized on nature's gifts without protecting the springs from which they flow.

Our obsession with money is evident in the way we normally speak of wealth, as if it could be measured by numbers in bank accounts and investment portfolios. But this is an anemic use of a word that carries a more robust meaning. *Weal* means wellbeing, so *wealth* is a state of wellbeing. Trace *weal* and *well* and *will* back to their origins, and you find a single Indo-European verb that means to wish or to choose. To be well, or to be wealthy, is to be in the condition we most desire.

Leaf through the pages of *Wealth* magazine or consult the "wealth-building" services of a financial advisor, and you will learn how to increase your pile of dollars but not how to become happy or healthy or wise. Granted, in a cash economy one needs a certain amount of money in order to get by. Beyond that modest level, however, what else besides money do we need to achieve a state of wellbeing? I suspect that for many of us, the list of things we most desire would include a thriving family, loyal friends, trustworthy neighbors, good work, wholesome food, a secure and comfortable home. Beyond our own private sphere, we might wish for safe streets, honest government, clean water and air, good schools and libraries, abundant parks and open lands, lively arts, a vigorous local economy, and a world at peace.

The grand old name for these shared sources of wellbeing is *commonwealth*. True wealth can never be wholly private, any more than it can be wholly financial. No amount of money will insulate us from a degraded society or a devastated landscape. Dollars come and go. Stock prices rise and fall. The only forms of wealth that endure are those we possess and care for in common—the legacy of knowledge and skills, the humane institutions, the settlements and farms, and the fruitful earth.

Just as we have taken too narrow and private a view of wealth, so we have taken too shallow a view of community. We speak of golf communities, resort communities, and online communities, as if they were places we could visit or leave at our whim. We speak of the scientific community, the religious community, and the international community, as if they were vast, vague, free-floating clubs we could join according to our professions or beliefs.

If we trace the word *community* back through *common* to its roots, we find that it derives from an Indo-European base meaning to exchange or barter. The prefix *com-* means closely alongside of or next to, suggesting intimacy. So *community* implies a mutual dependence and trust, as among neighbors who swap tools and seeds and stories, who return one another's wandering livestock, who look out for one another's children, who join together in raising a barn or harvesting a crop. In the original sense of the word, a community would be small enough for the members to encounter one another face-to-face; it would be grounded in a particular place; and it would derive its vitality from the circulation of goods, gifts, labor, and ideas.

The Amish have never forgotten the value of a shared life in a shared place. Before they take any action on their farms or in their households, they ask what effect it might have on the community. If it would hurt their neighbors or damage the soil or poison the wells, then it would be wrong, no matter if the action were convenient or profitable. Similarly, the Iroquois, when they meet in council, ask what might be the effects of their decisions on the descendants who will dwell in their homeland seven generations into the future. By posing these questions, the Amish and the Iroquois acknowledge that membership in community entails responsibility for preserving the health of a place.

To speak about the health of a place, as opposed to a person, goes against our customary use of that word. We talk about health clubs, health tips, health aids, and health professions, all with reference to preserving or restoring the fitness of an individual's body or mind.

But the word carries a larger meaning. *Health* comes from the same root as *hale, whole,* and *holy.* It means complete, uninjured, sound. While a man or woman, a horse or tree in prime condition might be described as healthy, so might a free-flowing river, an old growth forest, a loving family, a flourishing city, or a country at peace. We know, in fact, that a child growing up in a hateful family will suffer injury, as will a horse drinking from a polluted stream, or a tree drenched by acid rain. So the soundness of the part depends on the soundness of the whole. The health of individuals depends on the health of their households, communities, and homelands.

Like a healthy person, healthy land is vibrant, self-renewing, and lovely. It radiates a sense of integrity, all its parts gathering to form a resilient whole. We encounter such dynamic integrity not only in big wilderness but also in farms and forests that have been cared for through generations, in roadside ditches that simmer with butterflies, in streams that run with salmon, in schoolyard gardens and city parks. The radiance and vigor we behold in such places draw on the shaping energies of the entire earth, and ultimately, through sun and moon and stars, on the cosmos. People who live in daily contact with wildness perceive this nurturing energy as holy. So they give thanks for food, for trees, for sunshine and rain, for breath. They honor the springs of life. They realize that only by protecting Earth's body can we protect the health and holiness of our own.

The most provocative word we have for the love that a person may feel for a place is *patriotism.* As we use the word nowadays—especially in the wake of the terrorist attacks on September 11, 2001—it arouses images of flags, soldiers, cemeteries, war memorials, and MADE IN AMERICA labels. Politicians pose for the cameras against a backdrop of stars and stripes, while declaring that patriotism means adherence to their own favorite policies. Advertisers tell us that patriotism means cruising the roads in our oversized cars, riding airplanes to vacation spots, investing in the stock market, running up debt on our charge cards, all for the sake of the American economy. Pundits and preachers identify patriotism with voting or with pledging allegiance or with regular attendance at church.

What is lost in all these uses of the word is the original meaning of *pater*-ism, which is love of one's fatherland. We might equally speak of *mater*-ism, love of one's motherland. In either case, what's essential is the gratitude and devotion that a child feels toward the source of its life. And the source, here, is understood to be the land—not the leaders of the tribe, not the warriors, not the buildings or traditions of the clan—but the abounding earth, with its creatures and cycles and seasons.

Imagine what our ancestors would think to hear us call ourselves patriotic for dropping bombs on foreign countries, while each year thousands of tons of topsoil wash from our fields down the Mississippi River. Imagine what they would think of our bragging about the American economy as a beacon to the world, while our forests and lakes die from acid rain, our rivers run foul, and our cities choke from smog. Imagine what they would think of those who invoke national security to justify drilling for oil in the Arctic National Wildlife Refuge, while refusing to support more efficient use of the oil we already have. Where, in all of that, is respect for Mother and Father America? How can we be patriots without loving and defending the land itself?

Like talk about patriotism, talk about security evokes military images—again, all the more so in the wake of the September 11th attacks. The sources of public security we hear about most often are the army, navy, air force, and police. The sources of private security we hear about are guns, alarms, and bank accounts. In the name of security, politicians offer us trillion-dollar missile shields, the Pentagon and its legions of contractors sell us newfangled weapons, developers peddle homes protected by fences and guards, car companies push four-wheel drive, and investment companies exhort us to grab a piece of the rock.

But are money and military force the best guarantees of our security? The words we've already examined suggest that our ancestors thought otherwise. In their original meanings, *growth, resource, wealth, community, health,* and *patriotism* all reveal an understanding that the wellbeing of people depends on the wellbeing of the land they share. Deplete the land, and you endanger the people. Those words also reveal an understanding that security can never be merely private, no matter how high the fences, no matter how large the net worth. Damage the commonwealth, and even the richest and mightiest individuals will suffer.

The word *secure* is made up of *se-,* meaning free from, and *cura,* meaning care or concern. Think of all that would be required to free us from care. True, we sometimes need warriors to defend us against attacks. But we also need to know that our children can play outside without danger, that we can safely drink the water and breathe the air, that we can count on a supply of nutritious food. We need shelter that's dry and warm. We need reliable neighbors. We need to trust that our jobs won't disappear at the whim of global corporations. We need to know that we'll be cared for when we fall sick and when we grow old.

By these measures, tens of millions of Americans are insecure, and no additions to the Pentagon budget will free them from care. Genuine security begins not with weapons but with membership in a loving community in a vibrant landscape, a community able to meet its basic needs from local sources, respectful of the weak as well as the strong, devoted to the wellbeing of all its members.

The word *conserve* rises from an Indo-European root meaning to watch over, protect, or guard. Although it's the source of both *conservationist* and *conservative,* those who wear one label tend to be suspicious of those who wear the other. Both camps agree that some things are worth defending, but they disagree, often vehemently, over what those things are.

In America today, many people who call themselves conservatives defend a literal reading of the Bible, the authority of men over women, the freedom of landowners from legal restraint, the unimpeded growth of human population, the rights of gun owners and corporations, and the privileges of private wealth. By contrast, those who call themselves conservationists fight to protect wilderness, watersheds, forests, topsoil, and other species, along with the knowledge necessary for preserving the health of the land.

Where the two camps might agree is on the need to defend certain human values and inventions that have served us well through generations—such as close-knit families, small farms, locally owned businesses, neighborhood schools, frugality, simplicity, respect for the sacred, sound old buildings, moral responsibility, wise stories, and rich language. If we could agree that these are treasures worth preserving, then we might learn to cooperate in defending them. The cooperation would be good for both parties. Conservationists would be reminded that such human gifts are as vital as any wild gifts to the flourishing of our commonwealth. Conservatives would be reminded that no merely human goods can survive without the flourishing of wildness.

Some conservationists have shied away from describing their work as *stewardship,* because of the word's religious connotations. In the Bible, stewards look after property on behalf of a master—and the ultimate master of all property is God. As the Psalmist says: "The earth is the Lord's and the fullness thereof, the world and those who dwell therein; for he has founded it upon the seas, and established it upon the rivers" (Psalm 24 1:2). In the biblical view, a steward is one who takes care of Creation out of love and respect for the Creator.

But *steward* has a secular meaning, as well. The word is compounded of *sty* and *ward*, so a steward is literally one who guards the pen where pigs or other livestock are kept. For a farming community, these animals mean a supply of meat, milk, cheese, wool, fertilizer, fuel, leather, and bone. To be a steward, then, is a solemn trust, for the keeper of the sty is one who protects the sources of life, perhaps for a family, perhaps for a village, perhaps for an entire people.

Although the religious version of *steward* is ancient and honorable, the secular version is the one we're more likely to agree upon. Whether or not we believe in a creator, we can still feel reverence toward the earth, we can still feel obliged to protect the sources of nurture and renewal for our communities. Instead of guarding pigs or sheep, in our time we're called to protect the soil, the air, the rivers and lakes, the forests and prairies, and the whole magnificent array of wild creatures.

The last of the words I'd like to examine here is *economy*, one of the most potent in our lexicon. For the good of the economy, we're asked to put up with unemployment, tax cuts for the rich, swollen military budgets, the draining of wetlands, the clear-cutting of forests, the damming of rivers, and countless other abuses of people and land. But all such arguments rely on a disastrously narrow understanding of *economy*. The word grows from two roots, the first meaning *house* or *settlement* and the second meaning *to govern* or *arrange*. So economy means the management of a household.

When we speak of economy, how large a house do we imagine? What belongs inside, within our care, and what belongs outside? As commonly used, *economics* refers to the distribution of goods and services through buying and selling. If you study the discipline of economics, you will learn formulas to predict and track the movement of dollars, but you will not learn the effects of those dollars on the world. Whatever cannot be assigned a monetary value—such as the atmosphere, the oceans, the welfare of our children, the love of our friends, or the survival of other species—is excluded from this narrow definition of economy. By this reckoning, what matters most to our health and happiness belongs outside the house.

Our ancestors would surely have been puzzled by how much we omit from our economy. They invented this word before there was money to measure by. For them, to practice economy meant making sure that nothing was wasted, and that everything needed for survival was looked after. In a less populous world, they could afford to think only about the needs of their individual households and their isolated settlements. In our homes and cities, we still need to make sure that nothing is wasted, and that everything necessary for a decent life is looked after. The arts of managing a thrifty household are as crucial now as they've ever been. But in our far more crowded world, no walls can separate our homes and settlements from the fate of our neighbors or the fate of Earth. We must enlarge our practice of economy to bring the whole planet within our care.

Depending on how we use it, language may distance us from sun and seed and soil, as Rachel Carson warned, or it may ground us more firmly in nature. To gauge the difference, consider these celebrated lines from *A Sand County Almanac:* "We abuse land because we regard it as a commodity belonging to us. When we see land as a community to which we belong, we may begin to use it with love and respect."

Aldo Leopold uses the word *belong* here in two radically different ways. The first is economic, legal, and abstract; it's about claiming ownership and power. When I say that a city lot, a field, or a mountainside belongs to me, I set myself apart from the land, asserting my right to treat it as raw material for my own designs. The second use of *belong* is moral and emotional; it's about claiming kinship. When I say that I belong to this town or watershed or region, I'm declaring membership, as in a family, and I'm acknowledging my obligation to behave in a way that honors and protects the whole of which I am a part.

The first use of *belong* is about grasping, and the second is about being embraced. Thus the same word can either deny or affirm bonds of affection and responsibility between person and place. The choice we make between these rival meanings will dramatically influence how we treat the land.

The land does not belong to us; we belong to the land. Conservation begins from this plain and simple fact. But how do we persuade more people to feel the truth of it, to know it in their bones? Here's what the Kiowa writer N. Scott Momaday recommends:

> Once in his life a man ought to concentrate his mind upon the remembered earth, I believe. He ought to give himself up to a particular landscape in his experience, to look at it from as many angles as he can, to wonder about it, to dwell upon it. He ought to imagine that he touches it with his hands at every season and listens to the sounds that are made upon it. He ought to imagine the creatures that are there and all the faintest motions in the wind. He ought to collect the glare of noon and all the colors of the dawn and dusk.

A man or woman who ventures outside the human bubble and pays attention to a given landscape season after season, year after year, may eventually become a true inhabitant of that place, taking it in through every doorway of the body, bearing it steadily in heart and mind.

Only those who achieve such bone-deep familiarity with a place are likely to care for it as they would care for their children or parents or lovers. If we aim to nurture a practice of conservation, we need to cultivate this intimacy with land in ourselves, and we need to encourage it in others. America has been blessed by many storytellers who've helped us to understand our lives and our home places within the great web of winds and waters and weather, animal migration, glacial history, continental drift, and cosmic evolution.

I think back with gratitude to the work of Henry David Thoreau, Walt Whitman, John Muir, Aldo Leopold, and Rachel Carson, to name a few. Among our contemporaries I think of N. Scott Momaday, John Hay, Wendell Berry, Gary Snyder, Terry Tempest Williams, Peter Matthiessen, Ann Zwinger, Gary Nabhan, Janisse Ray, Richard Nelson, Robert Michael Pyle, Alison Deming, Barry Lopez, Pattiann Rogers, Rick Bass, John Elder, Robert Finch, Bill McKibben, Kathleen Dean Moore, and so many others.

If you want to learn how to tell stories that will inspire more of your neighbors to care about the land, you can begin by reading the work of these writers. Every community, every watershed needs people who feel responsible for that place, who know its human and natural history, who speak resolutely on behalf of it.

As we speak up for the earth, we should remember the exchange between Humpty Dumpty and Alice in *Through the Looking Glass:*

"When I use a word," Humpty Dumpty said, in a rather scornful tone, "it means just what I choose it to mean—neither more nor less."

"The question is," said Alice, "whether you can make words mean so many different things."

Clearly, we can't make words mean whatever we choose. Language is ornery and wild; it doesn't change at our beck and call. But we can work at restoring language, just as we can restore wetlands, rivers, and prairies. I've made my own small beginning at that work here. By examining a handful of key words from the struggle for conservation, I've tried to show how we might dig down through layers of cultural debris to uncover a buried wisdom. In order to bring the voice of the land into our councils and kitchens, we need to reclaim this evocative, sensuous, and earthy speech.

Two Stones

for Ursula K. Le Guin

A man turning 60 may lose perspective on time, seeing all change as loss, counting his aches as if they were worry beads, anticipating the chill wind of his last hour instead of breathing in the present moment. And so, to regain his grip on time, to console himself for loss, and to remind himself of the great story in which he is taking part, he may consult with rocks. This man is all the more likely to do so if he has been collecting pebbles and cobbles and shards since he was a boy delving in the glacial gravels of Ohio, and if, from his wide-ranging travels, he has filled boxes and bowls on his writing desk with a medley of stones.

In these days surrounding my sixtieth birthday, the two lumps of rock I touch most frequently are both gritty and gray, and each one fits comfortably in the palm of my hand. One of them is more than 300 million years old; the other is less than half my age. The older of the two is siltstone, plucked from a creek bed near my home here in southern Indiana. It was laid down as sediment in the shallow inland sea that flooded the central basin of the North American plate for hundreds of millions of years. Collisions between North America and other continental plates have lifted up a series of mountain ranges where the Appalachians now rise, each range in its youth towering as high as today's Himalayas, and each one in turn eroding away under the friction of ice and rain and wind. Some 320 million years ago, fragments from one of those earlier mountain ranges tumbled down rivers until the bits were ground finer than sand, and the slurry of grit was flushed into the inland sea, where it settled to the bottom, mixed with the fallen husks of marine creatures, and eventually hardened into the scaly siltstone I hold in my hand.

The fossilized shapes in my stone are mostly crinoids, an ancient class of animals with a slender stem and a flower-like mouth, more reminiscent of lilies than of their true relatives, the sea urchins and starfish. The stem was a column made up of flat, round segments, each with a hole in the center, like a washer or a candy lifesaver. In crinoid fossils, these segments often appear singly, sometimes in short stacks, rarely as intact bodies, yet each of these fragments once formed part of a whole creature, every cell attuned to every other cell, as fully alive in its moment as I am in mine. Even though my sample of siltstone is young compared to the age of Earth, and even younger compared to the universe, measured on a human scale it is incomprehensibly old. To curl my fingers around a third of a billion years is comforting, for it reminds me that everything flows, mountains as well as rivers, entire species flourishing and perishing, the hardest rock yielding as surely as a man's bones.

The younger of the two stones I handle most often these days is rough, angular, and surprisingly light, as filled with holes as a sponge. When rubbed, it gives off the faint smell of wood ash. It's a glassy mineral called pumice, which volcanoes have been making since Earth was new. This particular piece was formed on May 18, 1980, when Mount St. Helens erupted.

The eruption was one of the most violent on record, exerting a force comparable to five hundred Hiroshima bombs. It blew away the top thirteen hundred feet of the mountain, spewing mud and volcanic debris over hundreds of square miles in southwestern Washington, damming rivers, smothering lakes, snapping or scorching millions of trees, killing countless animals and plants. Fifty-seven people died, including a young volcanologist who was monitoring earthquakes in an effort to protect others from harm. At 8:32 that morning, he radioed his last message to the U.S. Geological Survey base, crying, "Vancouver, Vancouver, this is it!" Within minutes a plume rose fifteen miles above the crater and over the next fortnight winds carried the ash around the globe, coating all the continents with a film of dust.

Soon after the volcano quieted down again in the summer of 1980, scientists returned to the slopes, expecting to find a lifeless moonscape stretching away for miles in the direction of the blast. What they actually found astonished them. To be sure, there was widespread devastation, some of which is still visible today. But throughout the blighted countryside, even quite close to the crater, pockets of late-lying snow had protected shrubs, wildflowers, and seedling trees, which burgeoned after the thaw. Since the series of blasts occurred in the daytime, nocturnal animals had kept safe in their burrows underground, and they quickly emerged to resume foraging. Many aquatic organisms had survived in lakes and streams. Migrating birds arrived from the south after the eruption, and other birds flew in from nearby to take advantage of the newly opened terrain. On the stony wasteland of the pumice plain, seeds carried in bird droppings or buried by mammals soon sprouted. Even in the raw crater, wind-borne bacteria and insects began colonizing the cinders, and spiders spread their webs.

I collected my chunk of pumice in July 2005 from the shore of Ghost Lake, which is ten or eleven miles northeast of Mount St. Helens, on the edge of the blast zone. Some twenty of us were camping for a few days on a ridge overlooking the crater, mostly writers, photographers, and scientists, all of us hoping to gain from this ravaged and recovering landscape, and from one another, insights into the ways of healing. We had been drawn together by our curiosity about the volcano and also, I came to realize, by a shared grief over the damage humans are inflicting on the planet, on other species, and on our own kind. The burning of oil and other fossil fuels was destabilizing Earth's climate, even as our nation waged war in the Middle East to assure the continued flow of oil; the industrial economy was stripping topsoil from the Midwest, emptying aquifers under the Great Plains, felling rainforests in Alaska and Brazil, pushing to drill in the Arctic National Wildlife Refuge, poisoning the Gulf of Mexico, and emptying the seas of fish, while politicians and merchants kept urging us to consume ever more. We ached not only from these large losses but also from the wrecking of our home places, the neighborhoods and watersheds we love.

It was a relief to visit the slopes of Mount St. Helens, where humans bore no responsibility for the wreckage. We spent our first day together learning from scientists who had studied the landscape since the eruption, about how life has returned with surprising swiftness to the lakes, the shattered forests, and even the desolate plain of pumice below the crater's lip. A quarter century after the eruption, you can still walk among the silvery trunks of downed or standing dead trees, mile after mile of them, yet these carcasses have become hosts for new life, from beetles to woodpeckers. The lakes and rivers have regained their full complement of organisms. The violet blossoms of lupine, red bristles of Indian paintbrush, pink spikes of fireweed, and white buttons of pearly everlasting glimmer from the ashy soil. Everywhere the saplings of noble fir, silver fir, Douglas fir, and alder have begun to rise. Over the next century or so, if the mountain remains quiet, the trees will return. For the present, however, there is a greater diversity of life in this mosaic of habitats than there was in the closed-canopy forest that preceded the eruption.

This hopeful history kept our grief at bay until the second evening, when we sat around the campfire trading memories and songs. As the light faded, a trio of nighthawks cruised above us, calling and feeding, and Mount St. Helens turned rosy with alpenglow. Every little while, steam rose from the fumarole, so obviously like puffs of breath that nobody bothered to make the comparison. It was easy to understand why tribes that had lived near the volcano for generations called it Loowit, meaning Fire Mountain or Smoking Mountain, and why they told stories about the Cascade peaks now and again quarreling with one another, shaking the ground, hurling rocks and trees. The earth felt so alive in this place, we could forget for a while the devastation of other places.

Then someone told a story about the cutting of a grove of trees where he had sought refuge as a boy, another told about the young people of her tribe losing touch with their ancestral ways, a third told about dying coral reefs, and a fourth person, trying to speak, began to sob, a sound that seemed to well up from our common reservoir of sorrow.

Sparks rose from the fire, drawing my gaze upward into the black sky. I blinked and blinked, but it was a long while before I could make out the stars.

The next morning, several of us walked to Ghost Lake through a labyrinth of blown down and standing dead trees. These enormous, whitened hulks were mostly Douglas fir that had prospered here for five hundred years, since the last time the volcano had scourged this area. We paused along the path to nibble huckleberries and praise the fireweed. Our arrival at the edge of the lake alarmed a spotted sandpiper whose chicks were feeding in the shallows. The mother bird circled above us, keening, until we drew back from the shore, and then she swooped down, gathered her chicks, and led them to safety in a thicket of willows. A song sparrow clinging to a cattail whistled notes I knew from my Indiana backyard. The spires of a young forest, as dense as fur, thrust up among dead trees on the surrounding slopes. In the daylight, loss no longer seemed to be the last word.

As we turned away from Ghost Lake, I stopped at the base of an eroding bank to examine a heap of talus, mostly bits of pumice no larger than schoolyard marbles. My eye snagged on a bigger piece that was riddled with holes, the imprints of hot gases from the 1980 eruption. Only when I picked up the stone and held it close did I see that the pores on top, where sunshine and rain could reach them, were filled with moss. The green tufts seemed to flicker like tiny flames from the sterile rock.

One isn't supposed to remove anything from the Volcanic National Monument, but I persuaded myself that this lump of pumice, no larger than a hen's egg, could serve the cause of conservation by helping me tell the story of nature's recuperative power. So I put the stone in my pocket and carried it home.

Over the following months, I used my two stones to illustrate talks I gave around the country. The 320-million-year-old chunk of siltstone, a compound of mountain dust and seawater, served as a token of Earth's great age and ceaseless flow and perennial vigor. Portions of our own DNA, I pointed out, could be traced back to the crinoids whose lithe bodies, broken into fragments, were packed together in this fossil as richly as raisins and dates in a fruitcake. The siltstone also helped me speak about my home ground, this Indiana hill country sculpted by water from the ancient seafloor, the lowlands lush with horsetail and sycamore and fern, the uplands shaded by maples, hickories, beeches, and oaks, a humid territory favored by fireflies and tornadoes.

Using my pumice as a prop, I told audiences that the swift recovery of the devastated landscape surrounding Mount St. Helens showed just how resilient nature is—how inventive, persistent, and sly. It showed that the earth, like our own flesh, is capable of mending itself. This wasn't to suggest we should remain passive in the face of injuries, especially those that we ourselves have caused—climate disruption, habitat destruction, extinction of species, poisoning of air and water and soil—but rather that in seeking to slow down, eventually halt, and partially undo this damage, we could draw on the healing power of nature.

In between trips, I returned the siltstone to my writing desk, but I set the pumice among other mossy rocks in a damp and shady spot behind our house. If the local moss was happy there, I figured, the moss from the skirts of Loowit ought to thrive as well. Week by week, however, the green sparks in the pores of the rock dwindled, until they were no longer visible even under a magnifying glass, and eventually they guttered out. No combination of moisture and sunlight would revive them. And so my symbol of life's resilience became a symbol of life's fragility, or at least of its exacting adaptation to the conditions of a particular place. My stone was out of place; it belonged back on the talus pile next to Ghost Lake, downwind from the volcano.

For now I keep the chunk of pumice on my writing desk, occasionally picking it up, running my fingers over the rough surface, gazing into the holes that seem as lifeless as craters on the moon. If my travels should carry me back to Mount St. Helens, I will take the stone with me and replace it. The siltstone I will hang onto, for it belongs here, on this old patch of seabed we call Indiana. Between them, the two stones, young and old, remind me that Earth is restless, powerful, forever casting up new materials and forms.

A 60-year-old man is merely one of those ephemeral shapes, his passage all the more precious to him for being so brief. I feel a reverence for this wild, creative, mysterious flow of things. Our lives, our civilization, everything we can touch or imagine is part of that flow, a wave lifted for a moment above the current, and then drawn back to the source.

In the face of a voracious industrial economy, technology that insulates us ever more thoroughly from nature, and a political culture that seems indifferent to the long-term wellbeing of the biosphere, the hope of preserving Earth's beauty and bounty may seem foolish. Indeed, we may fail. Obeying our cleverness and our appetites, we may so disrupt natural systems as to endanger our own species, along with millions of other species. We are certainly losing ground right now; we are narrowing the prospects for our children and grandchildren.

But we exaggerate our power if we imagine we can douse the green fire entirely. Regardless of what we do, Earth will pursue its wild way, as illustrated by the ancient history of rising and disintegrating mountains and the recent history of desolation and renewal on the flanks of Mount St. Helens. We cannot save the planet, for it is not ours to save;

the best we can do is to honor its magnificent energy. If we value the living abundance that we all inherited at our birth, then we should do everything we can to preserve it. In this work of preservation and healing we are allied with nature itself, which holds no grudges, never becomes discouraged, and never grows old. Amid so many wounds, this knowledge keeps me humble, keeps me hopeful, keeps me sane.

The Warehouse and the Wilderness

The world is made, not of atoms,
but of stories.

—MURIEL RUKHEYSER

*E*ngineers have determined, by patient calculation, that hummingbirds cannot carry enough fat to fly across the Gulf of Mexico on migration, and that bumblebees cannot fly at all. Fortunately, neither the bees nor the birds pay any attention to the engineers, and go on blithely flying. Every spring and fall, for instance, the ruby-throated hummingbird, although weighing less than an ounce, zooms over the Gulf between Florida and Central America, a distance of five hundred miles, at speeds up to fifty miles per hour. The bumblebee cruises from blossom to blossom, gathering pollen, defying the calculations.

Some literary theorists, who reckon by words instead of numbers, have also recently calculated that the great overarching stories, such as those offered by religion or politics, cannot give real meaning to our lives, and that even smaller stories no longer work. They tell us that all narratives—whether found in novels or movies, in scriptures or scientific formulas, in TV ads or sonnets—are mere language games, power plays, impositions of order on the shapeless sprawl of reality. They seek to rescue us from delusion by dismantling stories and laying out the parts to reveal how arbitrary and deceptive these fabrications are. Outside the camp of theory, however, people generally ignore these proclamations, and go on writing, reading, telling, listening to, and living by stories.

I'm one who dwells outside the camp of literary theory—so far outside that I can't pretend to know much of what goes on there. I know scarcely more about deconstruction or postmodernism, say, than bumblebees and hummingbirds know about engineering. I don't mean to brag of my ignorance nor to apologize for it, but only to explain why I'm not equipped to engage in debates about literary theory. What I can do is express my own faith in storytelling as a way of seeking the truth. And I can say why I believe we'll continue to live by stories—grand myths about the whole of things as well as humble tales about the commonplace—as long as we have breath.

Eventually I'll work my way up to speaking about grand myths, but let me begin my defense of stories by giving you a simple tale. Drawn from an early book of mine called *Wilderness Plots,* it concerns a man who was himself a compulsive storyteller and who died nearly two centuries ago in the part of Ohio where I grew up. The title is "Love-Crossed Carpenter," and here is how it goes:

If you wanted carpentry work done in that part of the Ohio Valley, you hired Nathan Muzzy. He was the best man with wood in the territory, but he refused all payment for his labors except bed and board. While he fashioned wainscot for the parlor or a banister for the stairs, you had to listen to him tell about his misfortunes in love.

Everyone heard the same story, which he elaborated by the hour as wood shavings flew. He had graduated from Yale College, which was a rare enough feat. Even more rare, as a young minister he had received the gift of tongues, speaking to crowds of thousands in towns back east. Then one night at a camp meeting while he addressed the multitudes, his gaze lit upon the face of a woman in the audience and he could not look away. He could speak to no one but her. The crowd shuffled out grumbling before he finished his sermon, and that was the end of his career as a preacher.

He followed the woman home to her father's place. She would have nothing to do with him until he proved his love by building her a house. When the dwelling was finished she demanded furniture. And when Muzzy had turned the last spindle of the last chair, she married a New Haven lawyer, with whom she moved into the bridal house.

From that day forward Muzzy had meandered westerly, raising a cabin here or a barn there, paneling a room, carving children's toys. In every lodging he retold his story. By the time he reached Ohio he was in rags and his spine was bent. The only sturdy things about him were the hands and voice.

No one could persuade him to take money, or to linger after his work was done. Between jobs he ate roots and berries. People told of overhearing him in the woods recounting his woes in the same entranced voice—and in the same words—as he had used in their parlors.

When he was found, frozen, one December near the pond that was later named after him, his body a rack of bones, the local people buried him. On his last carpentry job Muzzy had been overheard to sing out, "God be praised, the Devil's raised, the world rolls round in water." What he meant by that, no one knew.

There was a great deal else about Nathan Muzzy that no one knew, or at least no one bothered to write down. The only facts about him that I could discover in histories of the Ohio frontier were his name, his degree in divinity from Yale, his prowess as a carpenter, his last recorded words, and his commemoration in the naming of a pond. I used to swim in Muzzy Pond as a boy, so these few facts intrigued me. Even more intriguing were those last words: "God be praised, the Devil's raised, the world rolls round in water." What would provoke a man to give up preaching, take up carpentry, move from tame Connecticut to wild Ohio, and leave behind at his death such an ecstatic sentence? And why, of all that Nathan Muzzy spoke in a lifetime, did that sentence alone survive?

There was no way of answering those questions for certain, so the best I could do was to imagine a story, drawing a narrative line from one bare fact to another, composing the fragments into a pattern. My tale is not the only conceivable pattern for Nathan Muzzy's life, of course, but it satisfies me; it makes sense of his wandering and his lonely death; it makes room for those haunting final words, without exhausting their mystery. In my tale, Muzzy himself fashions a story from his lost love, telling it over and over, in parlors and woods, as if to untie the knot of his grief, or at least to make sure his pain does not go unremembered. For a while, at least, and for a modest number of readers, my tale will preserve his puzzling words and the memory of his loss.

Like a woven basket or a clay pot, a story is a container. It provides a shape for holding some character, some act or insight, some lesson we can't afford to lose. It stores the kernels of past experience like seeds harvested from earlier crops and carefully saved for future planting. Each person we meet, each place we visit, each event in our lives, and for that matter the universe itself in its far-flung glory, all confront us as bits of perception and memory, inklings and intuitions, and we seem compelled—like Nathan Muzzy pondering his grief—to bind these scraps into a whole that makes sense. The sense our tales make will always be incomplete, limited by the biases and ignorance of the tellers, and yet, despite their imperfection, stories endure. They are passed down by word of mouth from generation to generation, or they're recorded in books and saved on shelves and opened now and again by readers curious to know what pleasures and insights these pages might hold.

I've opened my share of books in search of old stories or the makings for new ones. In a dusty chronicle about the movement of white settlers into the Ohio Valley after 1800, for example, I discovered the tantalizing references to Nathan Muzzy. In the same volume I came across so many remarkable figures and gestures that I wound up making story after story to contain them, until I had gathered the fifty brief tales in *Wilderness Plots*. Consider one more sample of these resurrected stories, "What They Told About the Beasts," which derives from anecdotes of violent encounters between the settlers and wild animals:

> Here is what they told about the beasts: On the slate ledges above Justin Eddy's place the men killed seventy-two rattlesnakes one Sunday. The largest rattler was hauled out and tormented for

an hour with sharpened poles. At last the creature clamped its fangs into one of the sticks and its venom ascended, by actual measure, twenty-two inches through the pores of the wood.

The last deer ever to be surprised grazing on the town square of Carthage was a sixteen-point buck, stoned to death by a gang of boys in 1819.

When Miss Sally Taylor lost her way one night in the Muskingum Woods, the wolves soon closed round, and she concluded all was up with her. The horse wanted to bolt, but she kept tight hold on the bridle. Then she crept under its quivering belly and sheltered there all night, screeching at the wolves when they drew too near.

Late one evening Lemuel Chapman lost his way in the woods east of his house while searching for cows. Afraid of getting further lost, he climbed a tree to spend the night. Not long after, he could hear his son Joel down below, saying, "Well, I guess the wolves have got Daddy." Whereupon the old man sang out, "I'll get you when I come down," thereby scaring son Joel nearly senseless.

In 1808 Kate Briggs met a bear on the path leading to the woodpile and in a fair and square fight she killed it with her ax, the wives of Ben and Gib McDaniels acting as umpires.

Upon hearing a ruckus from her sheep pen, Eunice Sheldon grabbed a rail off the fence and went to investigate. What she at first thought to be a large dog ripping apart one of her ewes turned out to be a panther. Without bothering to yell for her husband, she brained the great lion, and later made a lap rug from it.

The mother of Squire Crocker stopped her spinning wheel one day in 1820, to see why it was making such a curious noise. She soon heard the rattler a-buzzing beneath the floorboards. Her son routed his snakeship out and staved in its head. The length of it was six feet, two inches.

And so the war with the beasts simmered on. Within five decades after the first white settlers arrived, these animals were extinct in all that territory: elk, panther, wolf, bear, wildcat, beaver, black and yellow rattlesnakes, bald eagle.

Why would pioneers laying claim to a wilderness tell such stories, remember them, and set them down on paper? And why would someone like me, coming along 150 to 200 years later, weave these anecdotes into a new tale? Our motives, I suspect, were roughly the same as those of any storytellers, from any time or place. By telling stories we seek to preserve remarkable deeds or characters; we seek to amuse ourselves and our companions; we seek to trace our history onto the land and thus make ourselves at home; we seek to bolster our courage in a dangerous world. By sharing stories we celebrate bravery, ingenuity, and strength; we laugh at stupidity and weakness; we relish romance and lament loss. Through stories we reveal what we've come to understand about ourselves and the universe, we pass on lessons, we stare down death.

While death remains a constant, our understanding of the universe and our sense of how to behave keeps evolving, generation by generation, and we keep reading past lessons in a fresh light. Stories told by pioneers in the Ohio Valley from the early nineteenth century instruct us to kill any wild animal that balks or threatens us. By the late twentieth century, when I discovered these anecdotes in old books, wild animals had come to seem less dangerous than endangered. We have so thoroughly vanquished the wilderness, at least in the lower forty-eight states, that it survives now only in enclaves and only at our pleasure. And our pleasure is fickle. Not a day goes by without someone scheming up ways to make money by drilling, mining, logging, bulldozing, or otherwise exploiting the remaining patches of wilderness, without regard for the creatures that need those refuges. The pressure is so implacable that eventually it bends the will of politicians or judges, and the engines roar into yet another sanctuary. So in gathering the settlers' tales and fashioning them into a tale of my own, I revised the original lesson about triumph over the beasts into a eulogy and warning about extinction.

Passing within earshot of the skeptical theorists, I've heard them say that the notion of a biological species is only a social construct, and so is the notion of wilderness, and so is the idea of nature itself. If our language for speaking about the wild economy of the world is suspect, then any defense of "species" or "wilderness" will be equally suspect, and so will the stories we tell about "nature."

If the black-footed ferret or northern spotted owl disappears forever, have we lost anything more than a name? If oil derricks rise in the Arctic National Wildlife Refuge, or giant redwoods fall to chainsaws in California's John Muir Woods, have we destroyed anything more than our fond illusions about unsullied nature? If "nature" is a construct, a fiction we have imposed, through science and religion and art, on the flux of things, then a shopping mall is no less natural than a meadow, a taco stand no less natural than a stand of oaks. By this logic, to favor a prairie over a golf course or a swamp over a subdivision is to indulge in whimsical preferences that are grounded in language rather than reality.

While intellectuals argue over the meaning of words, plants and animals are dying wholesale, natural systems are breaking down, and the planet is becoming less and less hospitable to life, largely due to human activity. Far from questioning that activity, those who dismantle all our ways for speaking about nature reinforce the view that the non-human world is merely a screen on which to project our designs and desires. Wittingly or unwittingly, these antagonists of stories are themselves caught up in one of the great ruling narratives of industrial civilization. It goes roughly like this:

A long while ago the universe burst into being out of the void by accident. The primal energy cooled into particles, then vast clouds of these particles gathered into stars, and then around some of those stars leftover stuff congealed into planets. On one of those planets matter started clumping, by a further series of accidents, into forms that could replicate themselves. These forms kept evolving in response to random mutation and the stresses of the environment, until they produced two-legged forms that happen to write books and drive cars and play baseball. These two-legged creatures arrive on the scene with no more purpose, meaning, or mission than any other parcels of matter. They walk around briefly on this minor planet, amid random stuff which they name and manipulate and use as they see fit, and then they fall apart and become stuff in turn.

Such a ruling narrative suits the industrial mindset, because it places virtually no restrictions on how we should behave. If the world we encounter has evolved through a series of accidents, and we humans are accidental products along with the rest, there is no rhyme or reason to things, no pattern or purpose, and no underlying order to which we must be accountable. Humans possess no inalienable rights, only those we agree among ourselves to accept in order to make our lives more comfortable. And since these human rights are only conventions, like spelling, they may be ignored when honoring them would be inconvenient—in the case of poor people who suffer under tyrants far away, for example, or in the case of workers whose cheap labor fills our homes with luxuries. Other creatures have no rights at all. If old growth trees sell at a premium, we cut them down; if chimpanzees make good subjects for testing medicines, we afflict them with ailments; if wolves threaten our livestock, we slaughter them; if whales taste good, we hunt them through the seven seas. According to this view, the world is a chance collection of materials and forces, and we are free to exploit, reassemble, and consume them to satisfy our appetites.

For the sake of shorthand, let me call this guiding narrative the Warehouse Story. You can find expressions of it in the pages of *Fortune* and the *Wall Street Journal,* in press releases from logging and mining companies, in the imagery of advertising, in the scrambled quick-cuts of music videos, in the jumbled cornucopias of shopping malls, as well as in postmodernist literary theory. You see the Warehouse Story at work when patents are granted for varieties of rice and mice and other organisms. You see it revealed in the indiscriminate release of manufactured chemicals into the water and soil and air. You see it used to justify the draining of aquifers for desert cities, the damming of rivers, the poisoning of lawns.

Perhaps most vividly, you can see the Warehouse Story expressed in the genetic engineering of new organisms—the mixing of genes not merely from a single species, as breeders have done for ages, or from different species, but from entirely separate biological realms. The genes of fish have been incorporated into strawberries, for example, to make them resistant to freezing. Bacteria have been incorporated into the seeds of corn to ward off insects. Genes from jellyfish have been inserted into the eggs of monkeys to provide markers for the study of human diseases. We treat bits of DNA as if they were Lego blocks, and we build from them whatever our hearts desire. If the combination of genes in a given organism is the outcome of chance, then for us to mix the genetic alphabet into new combinations is only to carry on the haphazard work of evolution.

All of these practices are in keeping with the views espoused by postmodernist theorists. Appeals to an inherent and inviolable order in the world are mere fictions, they say, and the old stories that make such appeals are oppressive. But the discrediting of narrative relies on an overarching narrative of its own, one that describes the world as a hodgepodge of stuff waiting to be used or sold, as aimless and capricious as language itself. The moral of the Warehouse Story is the one proclaimed by billboards and TV ads and hucksters: "Get More Stuff."

I could cite many rival tales, but let me outline one that I will call, again for the sake of shorthand, the Wilderness Story. Here, in brief, is how it goes:

Our planet is a great community of creatures bound together by a web of relationships and the earth is a tiny knot within the vast web of the universe, which has evolved for some fourteen billion years from simple forms toward forms of greater and greater complexity. At least here on Earth, and possibly elsewhere, some of those forms of matter came to life, evolving into organisms, and some of those organisms developed societies and some developed consciousness. Humans, as bearers of consciousness, also bear a special responsibility to learn what we can of the laws that govern this evolutionary process, to align ourselves with the powers at work in the world, and to care for one another and for all sentient beings. Everything we do takes place within the great community of living things, and so we can measure the morality of our actions by whether or not they enhance the prospects for life—not merely human life, but the life of all creatures.

According to the Wilderness Story, we dwell in a cosmos, not a chaos; the unfolding of the universe is meaningful, orderly, and beautiful from beginning to end. Storytelling itself is an effort to discern and convey hints of that order and beauty. Such a ruling narrative places firm constraints on how we should behave. If we enter a cosmos that is elegantly and intricately organized, a harmony of countless parts, then we had better do all we can to honor and preserve this harmony. If the gift of consciousness means that we can sense what other people feel, then we must treat others as we wish to be treated ourselves—the poor as well as the rich, strangers as well as friends, those who live in distant lands as well as those who dwell next door. If not only humans but all species deserve the right to flourish, then we must curb our appetites. We must leave some land alone, some trees uncut, some waters unfished. We must not alter the seas or the soils or the air in ways that will harm life.

You will find some version of the Wilderness Story in the science of ecology, in the pages of *Orion* or *Resurgence,* in landscape photographs and paintings, in the press releases of the Sierra Club and the Audubon Society, in the practices of organic farming, and down at the roots of the world's religions. It's there in the teachings of Lao-tzu, Jesus, Muhammad, George Fox, Black Elk, Gandhi, and the Buddha. It's there in the writings of Henry David Thoreau, Aldo Leopold, Rachel Carson, and Wendell Berry. The Wilderness Story has been used to justify the reintroduction of bison and wolves into Yellowstone. It has been used to justify the creation of national parks and wildlife refuges, the restoration of wetlands and prairies, and the tearing down of dams so that salmon may spawn. It has moved people to lead lives of voluntary simplicity and to strive for spiritual rather than material riches. It has inspired people to fight for the abolition of slavery, the liberation of women, the protection of children, and the preservation of animals and plants.

In light of the Wilderness Story, it is both foolhardy and immoral to engineer new species or to drive existing species to extinction. It is foolhardy and immoral to keep expanding our human population and to keep accelerating our use of Earth's nonrenewable riches. It is arrogant to patent forms of life and turn them into property. It is dangerous and deluded to set ourselves up as the rulers of an exquisite, intricate, and ancient order that we can neither fully fathom nor control. Whether we call that order Wildness, Tao, Dharma, Spirit, Logos, Law, or by some other name, we find its traces and feel its force wherever we turn.

These two guiding narratives—about the world as Warehouse or as Wilderness—embody two contrary orientations toward life. Is nature our servant or our teacher? Is the earth a collection of raw materials and tourist destinations? Or is it a living organism, worthy of honor and praise? Are we separate from other creatures, superior because of our clever brains? Or are we members of the family of life? The Warehouse and Wilderness stories provide contrasting answers to such questions. Like any grand myths, they profoundly shape the actions and values of those who embrace them.

As an illustration of these stories at work, consider the wrangling over the fate of the roughly sixty million acres of our national forests that have not yet been carved up by roads. Those who wish to protect these last wild reserves argue that, since over half of the national forests and virtually all private forests have already been fragmented by roads, and since the proposed areas constitute less than 3 percent of the total land base of the United States, it is only prudent and respectful to leave these remaining public lands unexploited, as habitat for wildlife, as a reservoir of natural processes, and as a refuge for the human spirit. Those in favor of protecting the forests, in other words, appeal to the Wilderness Story.

On the other side, representatives of the logging, mining, oil-drilling, and off-road-vehicle industries oppose any ban on road-building in the national forests. To "lock up" these acres, as they put it, would jeopardize business and cost jobs; it would threaten the American way of life by denying us access to fuel and timber; it would deny citizens on wheels the right to go wherever their engines can take them; it would favor the needs of animals and plants over people; and it would squander resources by allowing trees to die without being harvested. Those opposed to the ban on roads appeal, in other words, to the Warehouse Story.

You will have guessed which of these rival narratives I embrace. My point, however, is not to persuade you to adopt my favored story, but to show that stories have consequences. Nor is it possible, as some theorists have suggested, to live without an overarching narrative. The claim that the world follows no script is itself a script, one that makes us the omnipotent authors, allowing us to treat the earth and our fellow creatures as blank slates on which we are free to scrawl our own designs.

It's difficult to see how anyone who has reared a child, raised a crop, climbed a tree, or suffered an infection could think of nature as a figment of our imagination or a blank slate. That delusion comes, I suspect, from living too much in language, especially from clipping and pasting and pushing words around on the screen of a computer. That's precisely what I'm doing now—tapping words onto a computer screen—but I leave my chair frequently and stir about, trying to keep myself grounded in the world from which stories rise.

I make a cup of tea and breathe in the fragrance of mint, thinking of the leaves cupping sunlight. I might spread compost on the garden. I might sweep the red oak floor and remember walking among trees. I might knead the dough for bread in a bowl carved by a friend from a sycamore log, and all the while I'll think of the friend, the sycamore, the yeast. I might go down to my basement workshop and fix a faucet or a lamp. Often I'll stand at the kitchen window watching birds at the feeders. In summer, I sometimes spy a ruby-throated hummingbird, that migrant so oblivious to the opinions of engineers, its wings beating seventy times per second. Unless the weather is foul, I often go outside to poke around in the yard, maybe split some firewood, rake leaves, or transplant wildflowers. If one of my neighbors is also dallying outside, we'll talk a while, catching up on our children, our work, politics, or food.

These excursions away from my chair slow down the writing, as you can imagine, but when I do return to the empty screen and begin pushing words around, I am in no danger of forgetting the stubborn and extravagant reality to which those words refer. The world comes first; it's older, tougher, more subtle, and more magnificent than anything made from language. So when I go wandering from the desk, I'm not avoiding work, as it might appear; I'm stitching my work to the earth.

One Saturday morning in January, I wandered away from scribbling this essay to go shovel snow from the driveway that we share with our neighbors. One of those neighbors was out there shoveling already; in fact, it was the sound of her shovel scraping the blacktop that drew me from my chair. She's a slender woman in her forties, always brimming with energy and high spirits, even though she works long hours as a physician in a family practice. As we flung snow, she told me about something disturbing that had occurred the previous week. She was examining a young man who complained of a cramp in his chest, and when he took off his shirt, he revealed on one shoulder the bold tattoo of a swastika.

The sight alarmed my neighbor, so she made an excuse to leave the examining room for a moment. Outside, she consulted in whispers with the other physician in the practice and with the nurse practitioner, both of whom, like my friend, are Jewish. They shivered to think of the swastika. This is southern Indiana, where the Ku Klux Klan once held sway and where bigotry still smolders in many hearts. A few years ago, the local synagogue was set on fire. In another recent year, a white supremacist murdered a Korean graduate student in our town as the student waited on the steps of a church for Sunday worship to begin. My neighbor asked her colleagues what she should do. Pretend she had not seen the tattoo? Tell the man to put on his shirt and get out? Confront the man about his ugly symbol? In the end, she decided to confront him, but also to treat him. Her colleagues promised to listen by the door of the examining room, and if they heard shouts they would rush in and tackle the man.

The man outweighed her by a hundred pounds, my neighbor figured, but that did not keep her from telling him, after writing out a prescription, how disturbed she was by that swastika. I'm Jewish, she told him, and your tattoo fills me with pain and dread. The man flushed, then stammered an apology. He had served time in prison, and the gang that ruled the cellblock made everybody get branded with the same tattoo as a sign of loyalty. Without the swastika, the man explained, he would have been beaten, raped, maybe even killed. It meant nothing to him back then except as a badge of protection. Now, as a man who had gone straight, with a job and a wife and a baby boy, he was ashamed of it. One of these days his little boy would grow big enough to ask him about the crooked lines on his shoulder. If he had the money, the man explained to my friend, he would have the tattoo erased. As he put on his shirt, he thanked her for challenging him about the swastika, because it reminded him of how low he had fallen during those prison years, and how far he had come in the years since.

"I was so surprised," my neighbor told me as we leaned on our shovels. "I had imagined a completely different story. I could never have predicted the one he told me, and it changed how I felt about him. Instead of fearing him as an enemy, I saw him struggling with the same needs we all have."

One of those needs, it's clear, is to tell stories—his to her, hers to me, mine to you. I returned from that conversation to work on this essay with a renewed conviction that storytelling is as natural and necessary to us as breathing.

By linking events, a story binds together a stretch of time and a portion of the world, something tidy enough to carry in the mind. It is a form of stored energy, like the sunlight captured in a chunk of coal, but unlike coal, which disappears in the burning, stories retain their heat and light as long as there are minds capable of understanding them. There are small stories—how my neighbor met a man tattooed with a swastika—and bigger stories—how millions perished in the Nazi concentration camps—and grand stories—how the universe came to be the way it is. Stories differ one from another according to how those links between events are forged and how far-reaching the connections are, but they all do this fundamental work of gathering and binding.

We crave coherence and predictability; we want to know how things will turn out. At the same time, we desire freedom and excitement; we want life to surprise us. Stories often dwell in the tension between a yearning for novelty and a yearning for stability. Children stroll into a dark woods, where they run into witches and wolves; the hero or heroine climbs a beanstalk into the land of giants, meets a bull in the depths of a maze, paddles a canoe through rapids, rides a rocket ship to alien planets; and by the story's end, each one comes back, wiser and stronger, rescued by wits or pluck or a higher power, to the safety and tranquility of home. Or think of murder mysteries, in which violence disrupts the social order in a thrilling way, and then clever minds track down and punish the culprits, thereby reassuring us that we live in an orderly and knowable universe after all.

Just how orderly and knowable the universe might be is an abiding question for stories. At the heart of many tales is a test, a puzzle, a competition, a problem to solve, a riddle. And that is the condition of our lives, both in detail—What do I do now?—and in general—What does it all mean? Many stories tell about finding one's way through a strange country or a labyrinth, and that, too, describes our predicament, for we need to orient ourselves in the world, to find a path. No other species, so far as we can tell, needs stories to find their way. The fox and frog and fritillary dance to the music inscribed in their genes, and this seems to be enough. We do our own genetic dances, of course, but often we must choose how to act without guidance from our bodies, and for that improvised dancing we need the music of stories.

If a snake frightens me, if a wolf or a bear thwarts my plans, should I kill it? If a crazed carpenter shows up at my door telling of his lost love, should I let him in? If a friend betrays me, should I work to restore our trust, or shun him forever? Am I my neighbor's keeper, and if so, who are my neighbors and how large is the neighborhood? Why is there suffering in the world? Why must we die? For these and countless other questions, stories offer us provisional answers. The answers can only be provisional because, like the findings of science, they take shape in the imagination and then must be tested, time and again, by experience.

Science no less than religion is an attempt to draw narrative lines between puzzling dots of data. A physicist and a prophet will find different meanings in a burning bush, yet both will find meaning. The formulas of science are miniature plots; piece by piece they build up a comprehensive story of the universe as wonderful as any myth. In everyday speech we use the word *myth* to name falsehoods, delusions, and lies. In traditional societies, however, myths are regarded as ways of telling the deepest truths—about how the world was created, the purpose of life, the reason for death, the paths for humans to follow. Myths are those stories that reveal what has been learned from contact with the depths of existence.

I don't pretend to have plumbed the depths of existence, but I have a hunch about why we're compelled to make stories. The impulse, I think, arises from the cosmos itself. The stories that emerge from us, through our minds and hands and breath, are one more expression of the wild energy that fashions constellations and planets and toads. If the universe is capable of loving anything, it loves patterns, flinging out one form after another with a prodigal inventiveness. Most of those patterns are short-lived, like our own bodies, but as they dissolve they give way to new creations. Our tales, our formulas, our paintings and poems, our mathematics and myths, our ballads and blues, the whole array of our imaginings partake of this shaping power. I don't assume we're the only storytellers, nor the most important ones, but I do believe we help the universe to behold, as in a million quirky mirrors, its own flamboyant unfolding. To hard-headed theorists that may seem a peculiar belief, but until I meet a more convincing myth, I'll live by this one, and keep on welcoming stories.

PART
2

Caring for Home Ground

The Geography of Somewhere

for Dan Shilling

If we are to build up a civilization
around ourselves in these United States,
we must learn to keep our beautiful things and
to look at them more than once.

—VACHEL LINDSAY

*W*hy do so many American towns and cities feel like jumbles rather than communities, without pattern or purpose? What it means to lack a sense of place was memorably expressed by Gertrude Stein. On a return trip to the United States after years of living in Europe, Stein visited Oakland, California, where she had grown up. She could find no trace of her childhood home, no durable landmarks at all, leading her to remark that she could not imagine settling down and writing in Oakland, for "there is no there there."

Whether Stein's judgment was fair in the 1930s, when she voiced it, or whether it is fair now, I can't say, since I have never set foot in Oakland. But her judgment strikes me as all too true of many American cities and towns, where any sense of character or coherence has been eroded by the forces of development. Uniform highway design, strip malls, cookie-cutter suburbs, manufactured housing, garish franchise architecture, and big-box stores surrounded by deserts of blacktop have made our settlements less and less distinct from one another.

European visitors have long complained about the monotony of America's built environment. After a visit to the United States half a century ago, for example, Italo Calvino observed:

> A few outings on the motorway are enough to give an idea of what small-town and even village America is like on average, with the endless suburbs along the highways, a sight of desperate squalor, with all those low buildings, petrol stations or other shops which look like them, and the colours of the writing on the shop signs, and you realize that 95 per cent of America is a country of ugliness, oppressiveness and sameness, in short of relentless monotony.

The mass media contribute to this homogenizing of America by smearing across the land a single, sleazy imagery whose overriding goal is to grab our attention and sell it to sponsors, and whose underlying goal may be to mold our minds into thinking as the owners of the media wish us to think. Chains of radio stations play the same music and recite the same headlines; chains of newspapers print the same articles; chains of bookstores feature the same books; cable and satellite networks beam the same programs from Florida to Alaska. Over the airwaves, on billboards and T-shirts, through computers and phones, the usual products are peddled coast to coast. As a result of these trends, we spend more and more of our lives in built environments or in virtual environments that are monotonous, ephemeral, rootless, and ugly.

If you happen to live in a place that has preserved its distinctive features, you may think I exaggerate. But for every idyllic New England village, for every Portland, Oregon, or pre-Katrina New Orleans, for every Santa Fe or Sitka, for every Beacon Hill or Greenwich Village or Chinatown there are hundreds of American places that have lost touch with their past, have cut themselves off from their surrounding landscape, have succumbed to the blight of sprawl. Even in the best-preserved places, the same corrosive influences are at work.

Every now and again, here and there, citizens will rise up on their haunches and defend their turf against invasion by Wal-Mart, McDonald's, or some other Goliath; but Goliath never sleeps, never takes no for an answer, never runs out of money or political friends, and most of the time the giant gets its way. So the homogenizing of America goes implacably on, street by street, real estate parcel by parcel, restaurant by office by store, and we adjust to this regimentation in the same way that we adjust to rising levels of pollution, congestion, violence, and noise. Over the past half century, we have surrendered to the tyranny of automobiles, as if their care and feeding were the central purpose of cities, and we have allowed our home places to become the colonies of global corporations, which bear no connection to local history, culture, or terrain.

The resulting desolate hodgepodge is what James Howard Kunstler has called "The Geography of Nowhere." Kunstler laments, for example, the way we have sacrificed our landscapes and settlements to the convenience of transportation: "The extreme separation and dispersion of components that used to add up to a compact town, where everything was within a ten-minute walk, has left us with a public realm that is composed mainly of roads. And the only way to be in that public realm is to be in a car, often alone. The present arrangement has certainly done away with sacred places, places of casual public assembly, and places of repose."

One cannot feel delight or pride in a place, a sense of belonging to a place, or a concern for the wellbeing of a place, if "there is no there there." So it's not surprising that the erosion of our towns and cities has coincided with a retreat by Americans from civic life. The two trends reinforce one another. Our cityscapes and landscapes turn into jumbles because not enough people are looking after them, and ever fewer people are willing to look after places that have lost their souls.

The retreat from civic life has been documented by Robert Bellah and his colleagues in *Habits of the Heart* and *The Good Society,* by Daniel Kemmis in *Community and the Politics of Place,* and by Robert Putnam in *Bowling Alone,* to mention a few examples of a growing literature. These authors observe that Americans are less and less able to talk about or even to acknowledge any rights or interests aside from those of the individual, and consequently we are becoming ever more reluctant to join together to seek pleasure or to serve our common needs. These trends coincide with the triumph of television, which purveys the solipsistic, hedonistic, ahistorical mindset we blithely call consumerism. The whole structure of modern life—solitary viewing of screens, isolation in cars or in cubicles, advertising's emphasis on personal gratification—cuts us off from communal experiences and public concerns.

Whatever the reasons for this cultural shift, in recent decades increasing numbers of Americans have been withdrawing from involvement with local schools, clubs, and cultural institutions; giving up their subscriptions to local newspapers; abandoning main street merchants in favor of chain stores; neglecting to vote and otherwise ignoring community politics, except to demand lower taxes. The burgeoning megachurches may seem to be an exception to the solipsistic trend, but they are in fact another symptom of it, for they tend to focus on personal salvation rather than service to one's neighbor, on heavenly bliss rather than earthly renewal.

And as we retreat from civic life, where do we go? Into the frenzy of private consumption, which often necessitates longer working hours and second jobs; into therapy of one sort or another; into drink and drugs and other chemical pacifiers. Year by year, we spend less time outdoors interacting with neighbors or observing nature, more time in air-conditioned cars negotiating traffic or indoors transfixed by the electronic never-never land flickering on screens. Those screens tell us, through programs as well as advertising, that our pleasure, appearance, comfort, and status matter more than anything else; they tell us that the earth exists to satisfy our cravings; they tell us that we alone, out of all species and all generations, are the ones who count.

In the face of narcissism and homogenization, it is all the more vital that we recover a sense of place. A powerful sense of belonging to our home ground can draw us out of our self-preoccupation and revive our concern for the public realm. It can help transform us from rootless wanderers into inhabitants, from consumers into stewards.

What are the qualities of a real place, a distinctive place, a place with its own history, culture, and texture? What qualities give certain places a feeling of character and charisma? What distinguishes the geography of *somewhere,* makes it worthy of a visitor's deep engagement and of a citizen's love?

To begin with, a real place feels as though it belongs where it is, as though it has grown there, shaped by weather and geography, rather than being imported from elsewhere and set down arbitrarily like a mail-order kit. The connection to geography shows up in building materials, such as the adobe of Arizona and New Mexico, the cedar of Oregon, the limestone of Indiana, or the pine of Georgia and Maine; it shows up in architecture, such as the shady verandas of the Gulf Coast, the passageways linking house to barn in New England, the silos and grain elevators jutting from the prairie horizon of the Midwest, or the steel roofs on the rainy west flanks of the Cascade Mountains; and it shows up in food, such as Boston clam chowder or New Orleans gumbo or Milwaukee beer or Kansas City steak.

A real place is also distinguished by a vigorous local economy, one that draws on resources from the region and on the skills of its own citizens. Key enterprises, from factories to coffee shops, reflect the taste and judgment of the local people who own them, rather than the dictates of distant corporations. Although such an economy may produce goods and services for sale in the global market, it begins by serving the needs of the community, for jobs and healthcare as well as for food, shelter, clothing, and entertainment. Dollars spent in the community circulate there for a spell, instead of being immediately whisked away to some remote headquarters.

Visitors will know they have arrived in a real place when they deal with clerks who do not wear uniforms, when they find in shops well-crafted articles whose makers live nearby, when they discover on restaurant menus dishes they could not order anywhere else. They will know they have arrived in a cherished place when artists choose not merely to live there but to photograph and paint it, to write and sing of it; when archaeologists and historians delve into its past; when naturalists keep track of the local flora and fauna; and when elders pass on all of this lore to the young. Wallace Stegner wrote:

No place, not even a wild place, is a place until it has had that human attention that at its highest reach we call poetry. What Frost did for New Hampshire and Vermont, what Faulkner did for Mississippi and

Steinbeck for the Salinas Valley, Wendell Berry is doing for his family corner of Kentucky, and hundreds of other place-loving people, gifted or not, are doing for places they were born in, or reared in, or have adopted and made their own.

A real place commands such attention and affection.

It also conveys a sense of temporal depth, a sense that people have been living and laboring here for a long time. The traces of earlier generations are preserved in festivals and folkways and habits of speech; in old buildings that have been restored and kept in service; in landscapes that are still devoted to orchards, dairies, woodlots, and other traditional uses. While honoring the past, a real place is not trapped there, the way Colonial Williamsburg, Plymouth Plantation, Dearborn Village, and other historical reconstructions are frozen in time. A real place is alive and changing, like any organism, gaining and losing residents, tearing down and building up. Yet there is continuity amid the change. However shiny the new surface of a dynamic city or town, it does not obliterate the deeper layers. New construction harmonizes with earlier architecture. New practices acknowledge older customs. Newcomers learn from old-timers.

Although a place like Taos or Tucson is in danger of being smothered by the effects of its own charm, the charm endures, and it has much to do with the layered presence of Native American, Hispanic, and Anglo influence, a tumultuous history stretching back over centuries. In a nation still relatively new, reminders of the past are all the more precious. Visitors crowd the streets of Concord, Massachusetts, to commune with the ghosts of Thoreau, Emerson, Hawthorne, and other worthies. Visitors stroll the avenues of Oak Park, Illinois, to see among the recent houses a handful of lovingly preserved homes designed by Frank Lloyd Wright; they flock to Philadelphia to behold, in the midst of flashy newness, the Liberty Bell or the gravestone of Ben Franklin or an eighteenth-century Quaker meetinghouse; they journey to spots in Kentucky, Indiana, and Illinois to see traces of

Lincoln, and they range from Gettysburg to Vicksburg in search of Civil War battlefields. Tokens of the past may be newly built, such as the arch at St. Louis commemorating Lewis and Clark's journey of discovery, or the reconstructed boats in Green River, Utah, modeled after those used by John Wesley Powell on his descent of the Colorado. We glimpse a past reaching back more than a thousand years in the architecture and lifeways of Hopi pueblos or Tlingit villages, and we sense an even deeper past among the ancient earthworks of the Upper Mississippi and its tributaries, as at Cahokia in Illinois or the Serpent Mound in Ohio.

Even when the history is troubling—as it is in the massacre site at Wounded Knee or the slave market of Charleston or the whaling wharfs of New Bedford or the industrial ruins of Pittsburgh—we are better off knowing the history than ignoring it, and each of these places is more engrossing for having preserved a record of its past. The presence of history, good and bad, not only enriches our experience of place, it also reminds us that we who are alive now suffer as well as benefit from the actions of our ancestors, and that our actions, in turn, will affect those who come after us. Americans need such a reminder now more than ever, as we add hundreds of billions of dollars each year to the national debt our children will have to repay, as we use up natural resources at an accelerating rate, and as we degrade the biosphere.

A real place keeps us mindful of nature, as it keeps us mindful of history. In the built environment one feels the presence of the living environment—in parks, gardens, bike and pedestrian trails, river corridors, beaches, urban forests, and yards given over to native plants, and in all the creatures, from crows to coyotes, that share the place with our two-legged kind. Imagine New York City without Central Park, or Chicago without the lakefront, or Madison, Wisconsin, without the arboretum. One cannot think of Lexington, Kentucky, apart from the necklace of bluegrass horse farms, or of Moscow, Idaho, without the rolling doe-skin hills of the Palouse Prairie, or Burlington, Vermont, without the shimmering border of Lake Champlain, or Denver without its view of the Rockies, or San Francisco without the bay.

Although we can't all summon up spectacular settings for our home places, we can make the most of whatever nature gives us. In recent years, Providence, Rhode Island, has uncovered the rivers that flow through downtown; Louisville has restored the riverfront along the Ohio, Indianapolis has built a string of parks beside the White River, Cleveland has become reacquainted with Lake Erie; and in doing so, each city has reclaimed some of its identity. Even if our home grounds are not blessed with big rivers or great lakes, we can support land trusts and local governments in their efforts to expand the amount of green space in our communities; we can turn abandoned railway lines into trails and turn vacant lots into gardens; we can plant trees along our streets; we can replace our lawns with native shrubs and wildflowers and ferns; we can grow food for birds and butterflies as well as for ourselves; we can create ponds and prairies in our school grounds, enabling children to play safely in patches of wildness; we can limit sprawl, so that open country remains within reach of city dwellers; we can shade outdoor lights and clean up the air and welcome the stars back into our night skies.

A community can also maintain its link to the countryside by feeding itself at least partly from nearby sources—often through farmers' markets, where local produce is sold directly by growers to eaters, instead of being shipped hundreds or thousands of miles. Each of the past five summers, I have helped lead a weeklong retreat on a farm in the Mad River Valley of Vermont, and nearly all of the food served at these retreats, aside from coffee and raisins and bananas, was grown in that valley. Before each meal, the cooks tell us the names of the farmers who produced the vegetables, fruits, and meats, and they show us the locations of the farms on a map. There is great reassurance, as well as nourishment, in regaining such an intimate connection to the

sources of our sustenance: this is how humans have always fed themselves, and how we will do so again, by choice or necessity, after the
era of cheap oil.

If you were to visit my hometown of Bloomington, Indiana, depending on the season, you could walk with me among market stalls
heaped with corn, fragrant cantaloupes, gourds the size of basketballs,
eggplants like giant purple tears, and beeswax candles smelling of
meadows. You could gather the whole alphabet of fruits and vegetables,
from apples to zucchinis, or a bouquet of gladiolas, poppies, lotus blossoms, and phlox. You could listen to musicians playing reggae, rock
and roll, classical, or Afropop. You could sign petitions, register to vote,
question political candidates, or volunteer to work for a worthy cause.
And you could watch all manner of people, from grizzled quarriers in
bib overalls to executives in suits to college students in cut-off jeans
to Tibetan Buddhist monks in burgundy robes, all milling together
and smiling, as they fill their bags and arms with bounty. They talk,
touch, greet friends, dandle babies, exchange notes and promises; they
shelter from the rain under pavilions or tilt their faces to the sun. In
those faces you can read the pleasure that draws humans together
into villages and cities, the delight in sharing words, food, beauty, and
laughter.

This delight in the company of other people, so evident in farmers'
markets, is another quality of captivating places. Unlike the private,
often exclusive conviviality of clubs, the conviviality I'm talking about
is *public,* open to people of all ages and classes and descriptions. A vital
community provides many gathering spots, from auditoriums and
barbershops and cafes to playgrounds and plazas and parks, where
people are free to mix with neighbors and strangers; the more diverse
the mixture, the more illuminating the experience is likely to be. As far
back as we can trace human settlement, our ancestors created public
spaces for the exchange of goods and ideas, such as the bazaars and

courtyards of the ancient Near East or the agorae of ancient Greece. Here in America, town halls and village greens helped shape the ideals of democracy. Insofar as we have kept those ideals alive, we have done so by creating arenas where all citizens can enter and all voices can be heard.

A shopping mall is a poor imitation of these convivial places. True, anyone may enter a mall, but the space is owned by a corporation rather than by the community. It is not designed to bring people together but to separate them from their money. The stores, which may be found anywhere from Seattle to Shanghai, bear no relation to geography. Rarely are the goods for sale locally produced, or is the food in restaurants locally grown. The recipes, like the window displays and piped-in music, have been imposed from some distant headquarters. There is no freedom of assembly, as you can find out by trying to protest the sale of sweatshop products or fur coats, and there is no freedom of expression, as you can find out by trying to circulate a petition against our nation's latest war. Unlike an open-air market, a shopping mall is cut off from the weather, the seasons, the cycles of daylight and dark; it might as well be a spaceship, for all the connection it has to the community or the planet.

In a genuine gathering space, people from all walks of life may argue and joke and swap stories and admire one another's babies and sympathize with one another's aches, all the while feeling at home. Indeed, such gathering spots extend our sense of home beyond the four walls where we happen to sleep. The true wealth of a community shows up not in the grandeur of private residences or shopping emporiums but in the quality of libraries, schools, museums, parks, courthouses, galleries, and other public arenas.

It should go without saying that we encounter real places not by gazing through windshields or by gaping at screens but by walking. Alluring places invite us to immerse ourselves, to open all our senses. Sidewalks become more important than streets, parks more important than parking lots, legs more important than wheels. On foot, we experience the world in three dimensions; we move at a speed that allows us to absorb and savor and reflect.

By comparison, the world presented by the electronic media is disembodied, stripped down, anemic, and hasty. The more time we spend in the virtual world, the more likely we are to forget how impoverished it is. A screen delivers us a patch of something to look at, and speakers deliver sounds to us from a couple of locations. Compare the experience of walking through a woods or a town square: not only do visual impressions and sounds come to us from all directions, but also smells, textures, tastes, sensations of wind or mist or heat against our skin, and the kinesthetic sensations from the movement of our body. In a woods or a town square, we are also surrounded by fellow creatures, our own kind or other species, and these, too, are centers of perception. We evolved to learn from and be stimulated by the full range of our senses. By comparison, the world given to us by television, video games, or computer screens, is malnourished—like a diet of bleached flour. To compensate for that impoverishment, the virtual world must become ever more hectic and sensational if it is to hold our attention. The actual world, the three-dimensional array of sights and textures and tastes and sounds that we find in a vibrant city or landscape, needs no hype in order to intrigue us.

What all of us long for, I suspect, is to love the places in which we live and to live in places worthy of love. Surrounded by sham and disarray, we hunger for integrity and authenticity. We wish to dwell *somewhere* rather than *nowhere*. The list of qualities that distinguish a real place from a phony one might be greatly extended. But I hope I have said enough to suggest why settlements endowed with a rich, deep, coherent sense of place might inspire those who visit there as well as those who live there.

Of course, the danger to places of great beauty and integrity is that they may be overrun by the visitors and dollars they attract. Too often, tourism is only another form of shopping, treating the whole country as a gigantic mall offering trinkets and distractions for sale. Too often, it is driven by a yen for golfing or gambling, a craving for novelty or scenery, or by simple boredom. If we're going to rove about the continent, burning up oil and jeopardizing our grandchildren's future, we ought to be prompted by larger motives.

Tourism can avoid being merely another form of private consumption only if it preserves and celebrates the commonwealth of the place visited as well as the place to which the visitor returns. "Commonwealth" is a venerable word that has fallen out of use in our hyperindividualistic culture. On television, in advertising, from board rooms and podiums, we hear incessantly about private wealth, but we rarely hear about the wealth we share. Yet the wellbeing of individuals and of communities utterly depends on that shared wealth—clean air and water, fertile soil, good schools and libraries, safe streets, honest government, a fair system of laws, an abundance of public lands, access to the world's accumulation of knowledge and art, and countless other blessings that we inherit by virtue of our membership in the human family. Insofar as tourism enhances the commonwealth, it is a blessing; insofar as it diminishes the commonwealth, it is a curse.

The sort of tourism we ought to encourage would show us the lives people lead together in a place, how they cooperate, make decisions, solve problems, enjoy one another's company, and look after their home ground. It would renew our appreciation for the security that arises from neighborliness and mutual aid. It would encourage us to think about our cities, towns, and countryside as arenas for our common life, and not merely as patchworks of private property. It would remind us that we are responsible for the care of our communities, for the health of the land, and for one another. In short, such tourism would educate us to become better citizens, first of our neighborhoods and ultimately of our nation and planet.

In America today, we need to recover a sense of the importance of public life, neighborliness, mutual aid, and the common good. We need to reassert the importance of citizenship as the sharing of responsibility for the wellbeing of our communities. We need to practice politics, not merely by voting every two or four years, but by informing ourselves about local, regional, national, and global issues, by attending meetings to discuss public matters, by communicating with elected officials, or by running for office ourselves.

If my hopes seem high, recall that I am now a grandfather. The birth of grandchildren set me thinking even harder about our responsibility to future generations. We have been given much, and we should feel duty bound to preserve the sources of those gifts. We should do everything we can to reinvigorate our waning democracy and to heal our damaged land. I believe that a renewed devotion to our home places might help us turn toward a saner, kinder, more peaceful and equitable world. That is the world I want for my grandchildren, and for all children forever.

Hometown

*U*ntil I was in my late twenties, I didn't know how to answer the question that strangers often ask one another in this land of nomads: Where are you from? I could say that I was born in Memphis, Tennessee, but my family moved away from there before I started school. I could say that I spent my school years in the country outside of Ravenna, Ohio, but my family left there before I started college. I could say that I went to college in Providence, Rhode Island, and to graduate school in Cambridge, England, but every time I completed a degree I moved on. So I really wasn't from Memphis, despite the accident of birth, nor was I from Ravenna, Providence, or Cambridge, much as those places had influenced me.

When I finished the last of my degrees at the age of 25, I couldn't name a place or point to a spot on the map and say, "That's my home." Not having acquired a hometown in childhood, I imagined I never would.

From England, my wife and I moved to Bloomington, Indiana, where I took up my first real job, teaching at Indiana University. When Ruth and I arrived in the summer of 1971, our furniture, books, bicycles, and clothes only half filled a panel truck. Scattered about the second-floor apartment we rented in a house near campus, our few possessions made the place look less like a home than a campsite. Ruth began foraging at yard sales to fill out our meager belongings. I was reluctant to buy anything more just yet. It would only be a matter of time, I figured, before we moved again, not merely to another house but to another town, another state, even another country.

Up to that point in my life, I thought it was normal to uproot every few years and go somewhere new, if only for more excitement or more pay. During the Great Depression, my father had left his parents' farm in Mississippi to seek work in Chicago, where he found not only a job but also a wife. The Second World War carried him back down south, newly married, to work in a munitions plant. After the war he landed a job with a tire company, which moved him and his family all over the country, from Tennessee to Ohio, then to Louisiana, Oklahoma, and Ontario, then back again to Mississippi. My mother wept at every move, yet she threw herself into each new place, joining a church, running for the school board, planting perennial flowers that would keep blooming long after she had moved on once more.

I took such moving about to be the American way. While growing up, I had read countless stories about pilgrims, voyageurs, explorers, cowboys, and pioneers. These were the venturesome souls, the pathfinders. By contrast, the people who stayed put—whom I read about in stories by Sinclair Lewis, Willa Cather, Sherwood Anderson, Mark Twain, and others—were bigoted, listless, and dull. At our most lively, I came to believe, Americans were a footloose people, always striking out for new territory.

So instead of breaking down the crates we had used to ship our things from England to Indiana, I stored them in the attic where they would be handy for our next move. I worked hard at my job, but I didn't pay much attention to where I was actually living. I knew little about the city government, the schools, the parks and museums, the local economy, the sources of our food or water or electricity. I didn't know what social problems afflicted our city nor what efforts were being made to solve them. A few of the local trees, birds, and flowers were familiar to me from my childhood years in the Midwest, but otherwise I didn't know anything about the southern Indiana landscape.

After a year in Bloomington, however, Ruth became pregnant, and the following winter she gave birth to our first child. From the moment I heard baby Eva draw breath, the alchemy of fatherhood began to work a change in me. I began to look around our apartment, around the neighborhood, around the town and countryside with a fresh awareness. How clean was the air that our daughter was breathing? How pure was the water she would drink? How safe were the streets? Was the library well stocked with children's books? Were there parks where she could play, museums where she could explore? If we stayed in Bloomington even half a dozen years, Eva would attend one or another of the public schools. How good were they? How large were the classes? Were the teachers well trained and well paid? And who took responsibility, inside or outside of government, for making sure these needs were being met?

Suddenly I was beset by questions about this place where my daughter had entered the world. In seeking answers, I began to see Bloomington not merely as a way station on my career but as a working community, with its own history, its own strengths and weaknesses. I met people who volunteered at the hospital or the soup kitchen; I met people who were starting a food co-op, people who ran a shelter for abused women, people who fought to save and rehabilitate fine old buildings. I met teachers who stayed on after the school day ended to tutor children who were struggling. I met businesspeople who gave jobs to handicapped workers and donated money to local causes. I met politicians who bicycled to work and championed public land.

Of course I also met or learned of scalawags and charlatans and deadbeats, who were always on the take and never giving back to the community, but their like would have turned up in any town. I could also see that, because of the university, Bloomington suffered more than most places from transience, as students flowed in and out by the thousands every year, most of them taking little interest in the community during their temporary stay. Indeed, the majority of residents, here as elsewhere, appeared to go about their lives without giving much thought to the wellbeing of the city, collecting their paychecks and their groceries and assuming that others would make sure things kept running. Still, in exploring this place with a father's eyes, I discovered there were many people devoted to caring for the community, enough people to steadily improve the quality of life in Bloomington.

About the time Eva learned to walk, my wife and I bought an old brick house within easy strolling distance of the courthouse square and only two blocks from a city park in one direction and a public school in the other. A mortgage hadn't kept my parents from moving every few years; still, it was a sobering step for me to sign an agreement promising payments for the next thirty years. I had been alive only twenty-eight years, and already I had dwelt in ten houses. Ruth and I could afford this house only because it was small and run-down. No sooner had we settled in than we began fixing it up, and the sweat and hours we put into the work strengthened our marriage to one another as well as to the place.

"What about those shipping crates?" Ruth asked me one day. They were just taking up room, and she didn't plan on moving again any time soon. After mulling it over, I took my hammer, dismantled the crates, and used the wood to build storage shelves in the basement.

The neighborhood had been settled for most of a century, so the trees were big but the lots were small. We pruned our trees, trimmed the gangly bushes, dug up the flower beds and planted them anew. Neighbors stopped by with starts from their own gardens, with casseroles, with advice. The people living nearby whom we hadn't met on sidewalks or in front yards, we sought out by knocking on their doors and offering gifts of our own, usually cookies or bread.

Before long, Ruth and I formed a daycare cooperative with other parents of young children in the neighborhood. We found another circle of friends who liked to share food and folksongs. Ruth located shops where she could buy supplies for quilting and weaving. I discovered the best places to buy used books and new tools. We sought out the Quaker meeting, to continue a form of worship we had come to know during our years in England. We joined local groups devoted to peacemaking and conservation. We called or wrote or spoke in person with our elected officials (a mayor who served for eight years lived around the corner from us), and at election time we posted signs in our yard to support our favored candidates. When meetings were held to discuss the future of the schools, the library, the parks, or the neighborhood, we always tried to attend.

Within a few years our second child was born, a boy named Jesse. His arrival only deepened in me the change begun with Eva's birth. Here were two reasons for thinking hard about the importance of staying put. Children crave stability, a known world that is stimulating but safe. They also crave novelty, of course, but against a background of familiarity. For infants, the parents provide such a known world, but as children grow they need first the home, then the neighborhood, then a town or city for space to explore. Ruth understood from the beginning that Bloomington could be such a nourishing space for Eva and Jesse, and I came to agree with her.

Running errands about town, often in company with the children, Ruth and I recognized more and more of the faces we met. We knew by name the clerks in the credit union and the hardware store. We learned where our drinking water came from, what power plants generated our electricity. We discovered where to buy sound lumber, where to get our car fixed by an honest mechanic, where to buy organic produce grown by local farmers. With enthusiastic help from Eva and Jesse, we planted a vegetable garden of our own, watching sunlight, water, and soil give rise to beans, lettuce, and tomatoes. After putting up bird feeders, we soon learned the feathers and songs of the birds that lived here year round, as well as many of those that migrated through. We camped in nearby state parks, we hiked in state and national forests, and before long we learned the trees, the wildflowers, and a few of the edible mushrooms. We began to read in the local terrain the effects of bedrock geology, the traces of glaciers, and the patterns of human settlement.

Gradually I ceased to think of the town as a temporary address and began to think of it as a permanent home for my young family. Ruth had never needed convincing. Her own parents had spent all but the first six weeks of her life in Indianapolis, just an hour away from our home in Bloomington, so she had grown up expecting to find a good place and to settle there. For me, however, the desire to put down roots came as a revelation. My own childhood experience, as well as the notions I had taken in from books and movies and television, had taught me that to stay in one place is to be stuck, to lack gumption or vision, especially if that place happens to be a small city in the Midwest.

During my years in graduate school and afterward, friends who

knew I aspired to become a writer had advised me to seek out a big
city on one of the coasts—New York, say, or San Francisco, Chicago
or New Orleans, Seattle or Miami—some place that readers had heard
about, some place where influential critics might tout my books, where
I was likely to meet filmmakers at cocktail parties, where a cab ride
could deliver me to television studios. And they also urged me to pull
up stakes and move whenever I saw a chance for more prestige or more
publicity.

My friends were probably right, if my ruling ambition were to make
a name for myself. But my chief ambition, I discovered during our early
years in Bloomington, was not to make a good career but to make a
good life. And such a life, as I came to understand it, meant being a
husband and a father first, and an employee second; it meant belonging to a place rather than to a profession; it meant being a citizen as
well as an artist.

Good citizenship begins with the right conduct of one's own life
and one's household, then stretches out to embrace one's community
and the surrounding watershed. Only by taking on responsibility for
the wellbeing of your place can you become a good citizen of a state,
a nation, or the planet. I know from the example of my own parents
that people can invest themselves in a community in spite of frequent
moves; but the more frequent the moves, the more difficult the investment. I also realize that people can spend their whole lives in a place
without knowing it well or caring for it, merely staying on out of inertia
rather than commitment. In marrying a place as in marrying a person,
commitment is the key. The longer you stay in a place out of whole-
hearted desire, the more likely you are to learn about its human and
natural history, to help preserve what's worthy, restore what's damaged,
and create what's lacking.

So as I came to recognize my children's need and my own need
for a firm home place, I came to recognize my community's need for
citizens who stay put. Most of what I valued in Bloomington was the
result of efforts by people who loved this place, either because they

grew up here and chose to stay, or because they landed here and chose to remain. I suspect the same is true of all flourishing communities.

I realize it's easier to stay put in a college town than in many other communities, especially if one has a job that isn't likely to be shipped across the border or replaced by a machine. While all places are in need of loving citizens, not all places are easy to love. I also realize that many people must pull up stakes in order to find work or seek an education or follow a mate. I'm not saying that staying put is invariably the right choice, nor that moving on is invariably the wrong one. I'm only saying that in our infatuation with the nomadic way of life we risk losing the deep pleasure that comes of commitment to a place, and our places risk losing the care that rises from such commitment.

Although our children have traveled throughout the United States and in more than a dozen other countries, they tell us they are grateful to have grown up knowing the location of home. Jesse went to the local university, married his sweetheart, worked in Chicago and Brussels, then he and his wife moved to Washington, D.C., for graduate school. They swiftly came to know the parks and museums, the bike paths and subways of their new region. Given their professional interests, they're unlikely ever to move back to Bloomington, but they know they can always return for visits to this house where Ruth and I hope to live as long as we can climb the stairs, in this town where we hope to spend the rest of our days.

Eva wanted to sample another part of the country, so she went east to college—to my alma mater in Providence, in fact—then she returned for graduate school to Bloomington. She married a man who had also grown up here, and whose parents live on the edge of town. Eva and her husband bought a bungalow a few blocks from our house, assuming one of those long mortgages that had so daunted me. A few months after she finished her Ph.D., Eva gave birth to their first child, our first grandchild, Elizabeth.

Since Elizabeth was born, five years ago, I have spent many afternoons with her. In fair weather, we often go to one of the parks, or we walk downtown to the children's museum, the history center, or the county library, or we stop for a snack at the food co-op, or we check out the house renovation projects in the neighborhood, or we amble through gardens examining whatever happens to be in bloom, or we listen to birds, or we study bugs, or we go wading in a creek, or we rest on a bench in the shade of some great tree and watch the crowds flow by, visiting with the people we know, here in our hometown.

On Loan from the Sundance Sea

*W*hy, you may ask, does a weathervane in the shape of a fish swim atop the dome of the county courthouse in Bloomington, Indiana, six hundred miles from the sea? The explanations that circulate hereabouts range from sober to silly. My own theory tends, I suppose, toward the crackpot end of the spectrum, but I will share it with you anyway, because it belongs to my private mythology of this place.

A fish, some argue, simply has the right contour for a weathervane, long and flat to catch the wind. Some speculate that a few of the families who settled the town in 1818 may have migrated to the hills of southern Indiana from Massachusetts, where codfish whirled upon rooftops. Some think the weathervane is modeled on the perch in nearby ponds, even though it's the size of a 10-year-old child. Some explain the fish as a zoological compromise between Democrats, who wanted a rooster, and Republicans, who wanted an elephant. Some regard it as a symbol of Christ. Others see it as a warning that the actions of government, including those carried out in the courthouse below, may be fishy. Still others claim that the blacksmith who is given credit for hammering the weathervane out of a copper sheet and coating it with gold leaf in the 1820s actually brought it with him when he moved to Bloomington from Louisville, and thus the fish hails not from an ocean or pond but from a river, the mighty Ohio.

My own theory is that the courthouse fish swam up out of our ancestral memory, recalling the time when Indiana and the whole heart of the continent lay beneath a vast and shallow gulf, which geologists call the Sundance Sea. As the denizens of those inland waters died, their shells and bones settled to the bottom, forming a chalky mud that eventually hardened into limestone. Around 250 million years ago the heartland was raised above sea level by a collision between the North American and African plates, a prolonged stony grinding that lifted up the Appalachian and Allegheny mountains, and Indiana has remained dry ever since. Although global warming may swell the oceans enough to flood coastal areas within the next hundred years or so, saltwater is unlikely to reach the heartland again any time soon.

Meanwhile, I like to imagine that the fish atop the courthouse is keeping watch for the returning tide. Since I'm imagining, I think of it as a salmon—a coppery sockeye, maybe, overlaid with gold—spawned in a local stream and now seeking its way back to the deep. Whether salmon or codfish or perch, it's a token of wildness, reminding us that our land is on loan from the sea and our own genes coil back through all our ancestors into those primordial waters.

When friends who live on one or another of the coasts ask me how I can bear to live in the hill country of southern Indiana, landlocked, high and dry, I tell them my home ground is not really so high, only about six or eight hundred feet above sea level, nor so dry, because rain falls bountifully here and streams run through limestone caverns underfoot. Why, the place is so intimate with the sea, I tell them, that a salmon floats in our sky and our buildings rest on an old ocean floor.

Limestone is the ruling rock in this place. It's exposed in road cuts and creek beds. It dulls the blades of plows that scrape the thin topsoil. Bloomington is ringed by pits where the buff or silvery stone is quarried, and with mills where it is cut into elegant shapes. The foundations of the courthouse are laid on limestone and the building itself is fashioned out of it, as are many houses, banks, churches, and shops around town, as are tombstones in the cemeteries and monuments on the courthouse lawn.

I delight in knowing that much of my city is made from the husks of creatures that lived and died hundreds of millions of years ago in the inland sea, just as I delight in knowing that our sun and solar system and Earth itself—the copper and gold of the weathervane, the calcium and carbon of your body and mine—are made from matter left behind by an earlier generation of stars. Although my city is more durable than my body, both are fashioned out of recycled matter, both are caught up in the surf of decay and renewal, both are destined to survive for a spell and then yield their stuff to new constructions.

At first glance nothing about the courthouse or the square that surrounds it, aside from that airborne fish, looks the least bit wild. The square is a patch in the latticework of streets laid out precisely north and south, east and west, part of the survey grid that stretches from the Ohio River to the Pacific. The Ordinance of 1785 provided for that survey as a way of reducing the unruly countryside into salable chunks. In America's interior there would be no more reckoning, as in the original colonies, by trees and boulders, rivers and hills; here the land would be sliced up into square sections as abstract as any proof in geometry. Today, a hawk spiraling over Bloomington looks down on a checkerboard pattern softened only by a fuzz of trees.

At the center of that checkerboard, on a block of lawn dotted with war memorials, flagpoles, and Civil War cannons, rises the courthouse itself, some eight stories high, massive and magisterial. The style of the building is a Beaux Arts mixture of classical elements—columns, pediments, balustrades, heroic statuary—capped by an octagonal clock tower and a mint-green dome. Ribbed like an old-fashioned football helmet and topped by curlicues worthy of a wedding cake, the dome gets its color from the oxidation of copper. The whole affair is orderly, stately, solid, and symmetrical, proclaiming to all who care to look that here is the seat of government for a prosperous and law-abiding citizenry.

We're not always so law-abiding, of course, which is why we need courts and judges and jails. No sooner had the founders of Bloomington laid out the town in 1818 than they built a courthouse of logs. Made of timbers cut from nearby hills, it consisted of two rooms separated by a passageway and joined by a common roof, a style known appealingly as dogtrot. Each room had a single window facing east to let in the morning light. A shelf in one of those rooms held the town's first library. The court met there in summer, the school in winter.

The new county, named Monroe in honor of the reigning president, soon outgrew the wooden dogtrot, and so the commissioners ordered the construction of a larger courthouse made from brick. The bricks were fired from a local deposit of clay, which was the off-scouring of rock from the Appalachians and Alleghenies. So the new courthouse, completed in 1826, was sheathed in a skin of baked mountain dust. Painted bright red with white trim, it soared from limestone foundations to a sharp steeple, up and up until it culminated at the very tip in a weathervane shaped like a fish.

A man named Austin Seward either brought the copper fish with him when he moved to Bloomington around 1820, or else he fashioned it in his local blacksmith shop. Whichever the case—the stories differ—he mounted the weathervane on a post that hardly budged in the breeze, so it wasn't much good at nosing out the direction of the wind. Before long the gold leaf began to fray. When the county once again outgrew its courthouse in the 1850s, the commissioners were inclined to retire the fish, but local voices rose in its defense. It was given a new coating of gold by Seward's son, and it was mounted on ball-bearings to make it more responsive to the wind. Back up it went on the enlarged courthouse, and there it stayed for half a century until the commissioners decided to replace the brick courthouse with an even larger one of limestone.

When the cornerstone for this grand edifice was laid in 1907, there were funds in the construction budget not only for the finest limestone from local quarries, but also for stained glass in the windows, murals in the rotunda, marble for the floors, cast iron for the balustrades, mahogany and oak for the railings and trim, brass for the lamps, and copper for the dome. But there was not one dime for repairing or remounting the battered weathervane. Once again an outcry arose in defense of the fish. Civil War veterans raised funds to have it gilded anew, this time by Seward's great grandson, and to have it installed in its rightful place atop the courthouse.

This limestone palace offered a room set aside where families could rendezvous when they came downtown. Friends would say, "I'll meet you under the fish." Enemies threatening lawsuits would say, "I'll talk to you under the fish." When folks came in from the countryside to do business in town they often picnicked in the shade of the trees on the courthouse lawn, leaving crusts and rinds on the grass. These scraps attracted so many dogs and cats and flies that the same commissioners who had slighted the fish in their building plans now had the trees cut down. This provoked another outcry, which led to the planting of oaks, maples, and sweet gums, which comfort us a century later.

A century later, the limestone courthouse still presides over the city, but only because of the hard work and stubborn affection of many citizens. By the 1980s the interior had been carved up to provide additional offices and courtrooms; the furnace had become wheezy, the windows leaky, the pipes rusty, the wiring risky. When a grand jury, acting on advice from the fire marshal, threatened to close the building for safety violations, some commissioners called for tearing it down and putting up a sleek tower of glass and steel.

Yet again an outcry arose, this time in defense not merely of the fish but of the grand old courthouse itself. By then I had been living in Bloomington for a decade; I had served on juries in the solemn building, had paid taxes there, had run my hands over its limestone flanks. I had come to see it as a symbol of our local landscape, quarried and shaped by local skills. I couldn't bear to think of a wrecking ball smashing all that labor from carvers, sculptors, muralists, stained-glass artists, masons, and carpenters. I couldn't imagine the gilded weathervane swimming atop a steel tower, couldn't imagine wishing to run my hands over the flanks of a glassy box. So I added my voice to the uproar and my signature to the petitions for saving the courthouse.

Fortunately there were many passionate defenders, including elders, students, business people, and some elected officials. When the council met to decide whether to renovate or demolish, those in favor of preserving and restoring the courthouse prevailed by a single vote. I rejoiced, and it seems the whole community rejoiced, because the restoration of the courthouse and its weathervane, completed in 1984, set off a flurry of renovations downtown. A hotel, a creamery, and the Masonic lodge were turned into offices. A train depot was turned into a Japanese restaurant, a funeral home into condominiums, a warehouse into an antique mall. A car showroom became a convention center, while another one became a cafe. The old Carnegie Library became the county historical museum. The former city hall was transformed into an arts center, and a nearby cinema into a concert hall. A one-time furniture factory, complete with skylights set into a saw-toothed roof, now holds the city hall as well as lawyers' offices and high-tech businesses, and the adjacent parking lot now hosts the Saturday farmers' market. Thanks to the markets, produce flows once more into the city from the countryside.

Many of the shops on the courthouse square have also been restored, and every single one is open for business. The old five-and-dime is now a bakery, the former hardware store now sells books, the one-time department store recently held a rug shop . Within sight of the courthouse you can find bars and banks, an adventure outfitter, a science museum for kids, a newsstand, a cooking shop, a photography studio, a recording studio, a furniture store, an ad agency, a realtor, a grocery. You can park where the hitching racks used to be and stroll the nearby streets to buy sporting goods, eyeglasses, musical recordings, hobby supplies, bicycles, clothes, jewelry, cigars, guitars, or chocolate. You can fraternize down there with the Moose, the Elks, the Masons, the Knights of Pythias, or the Odd Fellows. One shop will sell you the statue of a Union soldier wielding a bayonet, another will sell you a wicker motorcycle, and another will sell you a leopard-spotted brassiere. You can study yoga on the square, plan a trip, frame a picture, play pool, eat cuisine from Afghanistan or Ireland or Morocco, drink local or exotic beers, have your fortune told by a clairvoyant, get a massage or a manicure or a tattoo.

July Fourth parades, candlelight vigils, protest marches, noon-time concerts, political rallies, all focus on the courthouse. On Friday and Saturday nights teenagers cruise around the square in pickup trucks and jalopies, or they park nearby and sit on the hoods of their vehicles to gab. On summer weekends artists sell their wares from booths under the shade of the courthouse trees. Near Christmas, musicians dressed as Santa Claus show up on a fire engine to play carols on tubas, beneath a canopy of lights that stretches outward from the courthouse to the shops facing the square. In spring, about the time the water is turned on in the Women's Christian Temperance Union fountain, pink crab apples bloom along the walkway leading up to the main door of the courthouse. If you go inside on a bright day and walk into the rotunda and look up, you will see a golden light shining through stained glass, as if you were staring into the throat of a daffodil.

The vitality in Bloomington's downtown swirls around that cop-per-domed, silver-flanked, statue-bedecked, fish-crowned courthouse. This energy reminds us of why we gather into communities to begin with. We come together to share gifts, to practice our talents, to nurture and inspire and take care of one another. We come together to build what we could not make separately. Everywhere I look in the heart of my city, I see the handiwork from past generations now carefully restored. I see the results of our gathered powers. I see above all the courthouse, this expression not merely of our bedrock faith in civil society but of our actual bedrock, lovely limestone, a cake of past lives hardened on the floor of the Sundance Sea.

Big Trees,
Still Water,
Tall Grass

for Barry Lopez

*M*aps tell me that my neighborhood of low hills and shallow creeks belongs to Indiana, a state bounded on the south and southwest by the Ohio and Wabash rivers, on the northwest by Lake Michigan, and everywhere else by straight lines. The lake and rivers mark real edges, where you can wet your feet or row a boat, but the straight lines mark only human notions, inscribed with rulers on paper. The soil knows nothing of those boundaries. Birds glide over them. Deer browse across them. Winds blow and waters flow through them. Thunderstorms rumbling by make no distinction between Illinois and Indiana, between Indiana and Ohio. Monarch butterflies laying eggs on milkweed plants in our meadows pay no allegiance to the state. Raccoons and coyotes prowl through our woods and fields wherever hunger leads them, indifferent to survey lines or deeds. Sandhill cranes trace their long journeys high overhead, guided by the glint of water and the fire of stars. These wild creatures are oblivious to the names and borders we have imposed on the land. They belong to a grander country, one defined by sunlight, moisture, soils, and the tilt of Earth.

For years I have aspired to become a citizen of that primal country, the one that preceded all maps. I find myself wondering how this region looked two hundred years ago, before it was called Indiana, before it was parceled out by straight lines. How did the rivers run? How did the air smell? What color was the sky? What would an early traveler have seen in the forests, the wetlands, the prairies?

Trying to answer those questions, I spent the fall searching out remnants of land that have survived in something like their pre-settlement condition. And they truly are remnants, for less than 1 percent of the territory that became Indiana remains in our day relatively pristine, unaltered by saws and bulldozers and plows. I'll speak here of three such places—Donaldson Woods, Loblolly Marsh, and Hoosier Prairie. For shorthand I use their names, in case you wish to go look at them for yourself. But these refuges shrug off all titles, for they belong to an order that is far older than language. They remind us of our original home. They give us a standard by which to appraise how good or wise, how beautiful or durable is the landscape we have made from the primal country.

In 1865, just as the Civil War was ending, George Donaldson came from Scotland to a spot in southern Indiana near Mitchell, where he bought a stand of old trees, built a house he called Shawnee Cottage, and soon earned a reputation for eccentricity. What the neighbors considered most eccentric was that Donaldson permitted no hunting in his woods, no felling of trees, no collecting of mushrooms or ginseng roots. He didn't clear any ground for farming, didn't quarry stone for building, didn't charge admission to visit his caves. He made no use of the land at all, except to walk around and admire it.

What Donaldson set out to preserve was a scrap of the primeval forest which in 1800 had covered some twenty million acres of the Indiana territory, but which by 1865 had already become rare. In two-thirds of a century, nearly all the forest had been cut, the prairies plowed, the swamps drained. No wonder the official seal of Indiana features a man with an axe chopping down a tree (and a bison fleeing). One scientist estimates that between 1800 and 1870, settlers must have cleared away one and a half billion trees, an average of seven thousand acres per day. Most of those trees were never used, but merely killed where they stood by the peeling of a ring of bark around the trunks, after which the standing hulks were allowed to dry, then felled, rolled into heaps, and burned. For decades, the smoldering piles must have made the countryside look like a battleground. Earlier civilizations, from China and Mesopotamia to Greece and the British Isles, had stripped their own land of trees, exposing the soil to erosion and extinguishing much of the wildlife, but none had ever done so at this dizzying speed.

Resisting the advice of neighbors and the appeal of lumber merchants, Donaldson held onto his big trees. After his death near the turn of the century, a combination of good stewardship and good luck kept the woods intact until they were incorporated into Spring Mill State Park in 1927. The park map now identifies the sixty-seven acres of Donaldson Woods as "Virgin Timber," a quaint label that joins a sexual term for an unviolated female with an industrial term for board-feet. Measured in board-feet, many an oak, maple, walnut, or hickory in these woods is worth as much as a new car. Measured by their historical significance, by their contribution to air and soil and wildlife, by their dignity and beauty, by their sheer scale of *being,* these trees are priceless.

I have gone to visit them often, in all seasons, never without thinking gratefully of that eccentric Scotsman who refused to turn his land into money. As part of my search for glimpses of primordial Indiana, I visit Donaldson Woods on a bright, warm, nearly windless day in late October. Viewed from a distance along the park road, these might be any Midwestern woods, fringed by sumac lifting its scarlet seed heads like torches, but up close they reveal their age, with fat trunks set far apart, scant undergrowth, and a canopy rising 150 or 200 feet. Stepping from the parking lot onto the trail at the edge of the sanctuary, I cross a threshold not merely from pavement to dirt but from the realm of mechanical hustle into the realm of organic, planetary rhythms. It takes a few minutes for eyes to adjust, for heart to slow down, for mind to arrive in this company of giants.

Not far inside the woods, I approach a huge tulip tree, lean into it with open arms and press my cheek against the trunk, seeking to absorb some of its mighty stillness. The bark is so deeply furrowed that my fingers slide easily into the crevices. Even if a friend were to reach toward me from the far side, we could not join hands around the girth of this tree, for it is perhaps four feet in diameter at the height of my chest, more than twelve feet in circumference. After a spell I turn around, rest my back against the trunk, and gaze upward. Frosts have changed the leaves from supple green to brittle copper, iron, and gold. In summer, the shade here is so dense that only woodland flowers, ferns, and the most tolerant of saplings can thrive. Today, however, beneath a lacy canopy, the sun shines through with a beneficence of light. The most abundant saplings are beeches and maples, which will eventually supplant the oaks and tulip trees and hickories. The other common trees in the understory will never grow large—sassafras, with its mitten-shaped leaves; colonies of pawpaws, with leaves the size of mules' ears turned tobacco brown; and hornbeam, with narrow trunks reaching up like sinewy arms.

I walk on down the trail, passing among the giant columns, laying my hands in greeting on one great flank after another, seeking a blessing. Even the smoothest of trees, the beeches, have been roughened by age. Their gray elephant-hide bark has often been carved with the names and initials of lovers. Tony & Jill. Betsy & Bill. I wonder how many of those couples are still together, years after they left their marks. At least the beeches have remained faithful.

The fall has been dry, so the leaf duff crackles under my boots with every step. As I walk, spider webs catch on my forehead like stray thoughts. Several times I hear a ruckus in the leaves just over the next ridge, without spying what made the noise. Finally I surprise a deer perhaps fifty feet ahead of me on the path—a yearling that gazes at me curiously for half a minute, twitching its delicate muzzle, until it catches a whiff of man and then with a flash of white tail goes plunging away. Otherwise, I hear only the hammering of woodpeckers, fussing of blue jays, crows guffawing, squirrels scolding, and the distant drumming of traffic.

Even in drought, the ground feels spongy, for this land has been covered with forest since the retreat of the last glaciers, ten thousand years ago, and during all that time the soil has been gathering its dead. Many of these trees have grown here since before Indiana became a state, since before the American colonies became a nation. I come across fallen trees whose prone trunks rise to the height of my chest, their roots thrust skyward still clutching rocks. They remind me of stories from early travelers who often heard, even on windless days such as this one, the occasional thunder of falling trees. It must have been frightening to close your eyes at night in the ancient forest, never knowing when a massive tree, tipped over by the weight of so many years, might come crashing down on the spot where you lay.

There is nothing to frighten me here today in Donaldson Woods, no falling trees, no bears nor wolves, no poisonous snakes, no enemies of my tribe. I know how the fear would feel, because I've traveled in wild places where I understood, from moment to moment, that I could die. Such places hone your awareness more sharply than any small refuge ever could. Aside from caves and cliffs, where you can still break your neck, and aside from rivers, where you can drown, the only dangers left in Indiana are all in the human zone, in cities and schoolyards, on highways and factory floors.

Safe though it may be, I still relish this sanctuary of tall trees. I rejoice that there are no stumps here from lumbering, no straggling fences, no moldering foundations. This patch of woods is like a country that has never known war, a land where all the citizens can hope to die a natural death. The trees stand for years or centuries, until succumbing to wind, shade, drought, ice-storms, insects, disease, fire. Even after such assaults, the big ones often hold on for a long while, as you can see by the number of fat trunks bearing healed-over scars from lightning strikes. Of course we have left our own marks on these trees—from acid rain, alien pests, warming atmosphere, thinning ozone layer—but so far the obvious damage has not been of our doing. On leaving Donaldson Woods, I realize this is one of the attractions for me of primal country—that here one may taste the flavor of innocence.

Since there is rain enough everywhere in Indiana to grow trees, the only places, aside from a few prairies, that would have been clear of forest in 1800 were those where there was too much water, such as lakes and rivers and bogs. Even swamps grew trees, the species that don't mind getting their roots wet—red and silver maple, black and green ash, American elm, bur oak and swamp white oak, swamp cottonwood, willow, sycamore. On a misty morning in early November, sycamores lifting their creamy branches above the pathways of creeks are the clearest landmarks I can make out as I drive to the eastern border of Indiana, near the town of Geneva, to see what's left of a great swamp.

In 1889, a new bride whose first name also happened to be Geneva moved to that town with her husband, who ran the local drugstore. As business prospered, Geneva Stratton-Porter designed and oversaw the construction of a two-story log house with ample room for children, on a lot not far from the swamp. Against her husband's and neighbors' advice, she began to explore the thirteen thousand acres of wetland forest, braving the snakes and mosquitoes and desperados that flourished there. If her husband was worried about her safety, she told him, he was welcome to tag along. He often did, carrying her specimen boxes. Fascinated by the secret life of the swamp, Gene Stratton-Porter taught herself the newfangled science of photography in order to record the moths, butterflies, and birds; she painted the marshy landscape on canvas; and she wrote a series of books, including *Music of the Wild* and *A Girl of the Limberlost,* which would eventually carry the name of this place to millions of readers around the world.

Limberlost Swamp was a gift of the glaciers, which leveled out this borderland between Indiana and Ohio, covered it with rich soils, and left it soaking wet. Such flat country is a confusing place for water. Some of it flows northeast toward Lake Erie, and thence by way of the St. Lawrence into the Atlantic; some flows southwest toward the Ohio River, and thence by way of the Mississippi to the Gulf of Mexico; much of the water simply stays here, not inclined to go anywhere. At least, much of it would stay here, had the contemporaries of Gene Stratton-Porter not dug so many drainage ditches and laid so many tiles, leading the water into one or another of the many rivers that pass through this region—the Wabash, Mississenewa, Salamonie, St. Mary's, Flatrock, Maumee, Beaver, Whitewater, White, and St. Joseph, among others.

The draining of the Limberlost had only just begun when Stratton-Porter arrived in Geneva, yet by 1913, when she left there for another small town in northern Indiana, the swamp was all but dry. She grieved over that loss, even years later when she moved to Hollywood to over-see the translation of several of her novels into films. The destruction of the swamp made many people rich—from cutting timber, pumping oil out of the drained land, and farming the deep black soil—and you can still see evidence of that wealth in the size of the houses thereabouts. Stratton-Porter herself grew rich from film contracts and the sale of her books, the best of them celebrating that rank, fertile, mysterious wetland.

On the damp November morning of my visit I expect to see noth-ing of the grand, primeval swamp, but instead look forward to seeing a small vestige of it called Loblolly Marsh, a 428-acre preserve where the ditches have been dammed, the tiles plugged, and the waters have be-gun to gather once more. Today they're gathering all the more quickly, because the mist has turned to drizzle. "Loblolly" comes from a Miami word meaning "stinking river," a reference to the sulfurous smell of marsh gas. The only smells I notice on climbing out of my car are the perfume of decaying grass and the meaty aroma of mud. My boots are soon black from the succulent mud as I make my way into the depths of the marsh along a trail pocked by the prints of horseshoes and deer hooves.

On such a morning, with the grasses on either side of the path bent down by rain, bare trees looming on the horizon like burnt matches, and the calls of geese filtering down from the gray sky, it's easy to imag-ine that the glaciers have only just withdrawn. There is a damp chill in the air. The earth yields beneath my feet. This might be tundra, roll-ing away far to the north, browsed by musk oxen, woolly mammoths, ground sloths, and elk. Even bent over by rain, the tawny foxtail grass reaches higher than my waist, the rusty big bluestem reaches above my shoulders. As I walk, my elbows brush the curled-up heads of Queen

Anne's lace, the spiky crowns of thistles, the drooping fronds of gold-enrod. Here and there, burst milkweed pods spill their downy seeds. The wet kettle holes are choked with sedges and rushes and blowsy cattails. In a few months these holes will ring with the mating calls of spring peepers and western chorus frogs, but right now they yield only a few, forlorn chirps from crickets. The sound of drizzle stroking the lush vegetation is soft and caressing, like a brush in thick hair.

As I come within sight of a shallow pond at the heart of the preserve, I startle a great blue heron that has been feeding there. With a squawk of alarm and a frantic beating of wings, the stately bird rises into the mist and flaps away, its neck drawn back into a tense curve, its long legs trailing. I am dismayed by this undignified haste. I want to assure the heron that I mean no harm. Yet my kind has been harming its kind for hundreds of years, not by hunting so much as by destroying wetlands. Here in the Limberlost, just over a century ago, a great blue heron could have fed anywhere among thousands of acres of prime habitat; now it must wade in ditches laced with agrichemicals, in scattered kettle holes, or in rare ponds, like this one I stand beside in Loblolly Marsh.

Rain dimples the surface of the pond between tussocks of willows and sedges. Beyond a palisade of cattails on the far shore, beyond a rolling expanse of grass, the horizon is rimmed by a line of trees, their branches reaching like frayed nerves into the leaden sky. My own nerves are soothed by the rain, by the prospect of water lingering here, by the resilience of this land.

In the mud at my feet I find the four-toed prints of a muskrat, the neat line of paw prints from a fox, and the splayed tracks of a raccoon that resemble the tiny hand prints of a crawling child. There are many other scrawls I cannot make out, for these wet places attract whatever flies or creeps, whatever runs or leaps. I see no beaver tracks, but I know that refuge managers have recently had to dismantle some beaver dams in the drainage ditches, to keep the nearby fields from flooding.

I imagine that Gene Stratton-Porter would be delighted to learn that part of her beloved swamp is being restored, that herons and muskrats are feeding here, that wildness is returning to Loblolly Marsh.

Wildness alone would not have sustained the third sample of primordial Indiana that I visit, a prairie in Lake County, up in the northwestern corner of the state near the steel mills of Gary and the skyscrapers of Chicago. At some five hundred acres, never plowed nor paved, Hoosier Prairie is the largest remnant of the grasslands that once covered a few million acres of Indiana. Prairies out on the Great Plains were kept free of trees by a drier climate, but here in the well-watered east they were more often kept open by fire. Lightning might account for some of the fires, but others were deliberately set by the native people—in this region, mainly the Potawatomi, Kaskaskia, and Miami—who knew that clearings improve hunting.

The only hunter I meet on my visit to Hoosier Prairie is a red-tailed hawk, which spirals high overhead with barely a tilt of its wings. This day in late November is unseasonably mild and the sky is clear, so the sun beating down on these russet fields heats the soil and sends up a column of warm air, and that is what the hawk is riding, on the lookout for a meal. I pick up a handful of soil and stir it in my palm, a grainy mixture of sand and loam the color of bittersweet chocolate. Where I'm standing was underwater until about nine thousand years ago, when a vast inland sea formed of glacial meltwater gradually shrank back toward the present shoreline of Lake Michigan. The sand most likely descends from bedrock in Canada by way of grinding glaciers and pounding waves; the loam is a legacy from countless generations of prairie plants.

The plants I see on my walk today have lost their sap and most of their color. Aside from the golden leaves of willows and cottonwoods and the carmine leaves of blackberry, the prairie is now a medley of buff and bronze. From the stems and seed heads I can make out downy sunflower, blazing star, leadplant, rattlesnake master, wild quinine, wild indigo. In the low spots that stay damp year round, I find cattails and cordgrass and sedges. Observers with far more knowledge than I possess have counted some 350 species of plants in this vibrant spot. As at Loblolly Marsh, here the tallest grass is big bluestem, which even this late in the season still rises higher than my head. At midsummer a traveler in this tall grass would be able to see no more than a few feet ahead except by climbing a tree.

The only trees stout enough to hold a climber at Hoosier Prairie are oaks, mostly black oaks with a scattering of white. The big ones grow in clusters with a throng of saplings crowding their trunks, and the clusters are widely spaced over the prairie with grassland in between, creating a distinctive type of landscape known as oak savanna. The leaves clinging to the black oaks appear to have been cut from old leather; the white oak leaves are the ruby shade of cooked cranberries. It's clear from the abundance of saplings that the savanna would soon give way to dense woods if it were not periodically burned.

These days the fires are set by crews from the Department of Natural Resources, usually in late fall or early spring. A charred swath perhaps ten feet wide between the prairie and an adjoining field shows that preparations have begun for a larger burn. The big oaks can survive periodic fire thanks to deep tap roots and thick bark. The other prairie plants are likewise adapted to fire, drought, hot summers, cold winters, and grazing, because they store their vitality underground, in roots, rhizomes, bulbs, tubers, and corms. Roots may extend more than a dozen feet down, and they may stretch out horizontally ten or twenty feet from the parent plant.

By midday the heat has made me peel down to a T-shirt, and I am having trouble believing it's nearly December. A brisk wind from the southwest rattles dry leaves on the cottonwoods, like a fluttering of bangles. The hawk spins round and round beneath the implausible sun. Much higher up, the silver needle of a jetliner pierces the blue. Nothing else moves in the sky except blown leaves, crows, and a scarf of star-lings. In spring I would see yellowthroats, goldfinches, tree swallows, swamp sparrows, woodcocks doing their sky dance. For now, in spite of the heat, the land is locked down, the migrants have flown south, the crickets and cicadas have fallen silent, the juices have poured back into the earth. Today the hawk will have to make do with white-footed mice and meadow voles.

Earlier frosts have curled the fronds of bracken and the bushy sweet fern. These are northern species, hanging on since the retreat of the glaciers in this damp, fire-prone land. I crush a handful of sweet fern and tuck it under the shoulder strap of my backpack so that I can smell it as I walk, like the clean fragrance of dried hay. I need this reminder of the earth's own potent smell, because the longer I stay here in Hoosier Prairie, the more I taste the murk of steel mills and refineries on the breeze. Even from the center of the refuge I can see, beyond a scrim of trees, the gleaming white tanks of an oil storage depot. During my visit I never cease to hear the grinding of heavy machinery, bulldozers and trucks and trains, as implacable as any glacier.

In the gravel parking lot I start up my own machine to drive home, adding my fumes to the air, adding my bit to the global warming that may help account for the crazy heat of this late November day. Every lot I pass on the road bordering the refuge is either listed for sale, torn up for construction, or already occupied by pavement and stores. So much dust blows across the road from new building sites that many cars approaching me have their headlights on. I turn on mine as well. It's 3 PM. The only clouds in the sky are ones we've made.

Off and on this fall during my search for remnants of primordial In-diana, a muscle in my chest would twitch. The sensation was not pain-ful, not especially worrisome, merely a light tremor as if a bird were shivering under the skin. When the twitching recurs this morning, the last day of the year, I wonder if the troubled muscle might be my heart.

Cold weather has come at last. I look out on a fresh snowfall—barely an inch deep but enough to renew the complexion of things. I welcome the change, even though the white coating can't hide a history of loss.

In 1800, the grasslands that we glimpse now in tiny scraps would have stretched westward to the Great Plains; the glacial wetlands that we've almost entirely drained would have stretched north to the Great Lakes and beyond, up to the ice-gouged vicinity of Hudson Bay; the hardwood forest that we've reduced to rare pockets of big trees would have stretched eastward all the way to the Atlantic and south into the Appalachian Mountains. Bison, bears, lions, wolves, passenger pigeons, Carolina parakeets, and countless other animals dwelt here in astounding numbers. This original abundance, thousands of years in the making, we have all but used up in two centuries.

I admit to feeling dismay over much of what we've done to this country—the clear-cuts, strip mines, eroded fields, fouled rivers, billboards, smokestacks, used car lots, scourged rights-of-way for power lines, junkyards, animals flattened on roads, pastures grazed down to bare dirt, microwave towers looming on the horizon, dull, boxy buildings painted garish colors plopped down in the midst of parking lots, scraps of plastic blown against fences. I know I am party to this havoc. I live in a heated house; I burn coal to write these words. I could recite apologies for this human landscape, naming the energies and appetites that have brought it to pass, but it already has more than enough defenders. What so many people call progress will get along fine without any praise from me.

I speak instead for the original country, on which our survival and the survival of all other species ultimately depend. Our bodies, our families, our communities cannot be healthy in the long term except in a healthy land, and we can't measure what health means without looking at places like Hoosier Prairie, Loblolly Marsh, and Donaldson Woods. I seek out patches of wilderness because they represent an order, a beauty, an integrity from which everything human and nonhuman has descended. These fragments of primordial Indiana are refuges not only for the plants and animals that occupied this land long before we came, but also for us. I've kept a token from each of the places I visited—a curl of sycamore bark, the furry spike of a cattail, a handful of sweet fern. Touching one by one these talismans of the primal country, I think of those roots lacing through the black soil of the prairie, beneath the swamp, beneath the woods. I remind myself of all that buried strength.

Limberlost

It is my belief that to do strong work any writer
must stick to the things he truly knows, the simple,
common things of life as he has lived them.
So I stick to Indiana.

—GENE STRATTON-PORTER

*W*ith a startled scrawk and a fluster of wings, a great blue heron lurches into the air and goes flapping away, legs trailing behind like the tail of a kite. The bird's hasty exit roils the muddy broth of a pond where it was feeding. Ignoring the commotion, a pair of coots and a clutch of mallards cruise on among the cattails and rushes. A part of me older than my own body wakes and stirs.

The man who has led me to the lip of this pond grins broadly, for Ken Brunswick delights in the company of birds and gathered water.

For more than a century, this glacial pothole and the surrounding lowlands were drained by a network of ditches and buried pipes known as tiles. Water gathers here now because some of those tiles have been plugged and some ditches have been filled, thanks to the efforts of Brunswick and a few hundred other dedicated people, all of them inspired, directly or indirectly, by the books of Gene Stratton-Porter, a best-selling author who flourished here on the eastern edge of Indiana a hundred years ago. She lured me to this place by her photographs and words. I have come to Loblolly Marsh to see a remnant of the vast, magnificent, vanished wetland that Stratton-Porter made known to readers around the world—the Limberlost Swamp. As a writer, I have also come here to see how words on a page can move citizens to reclaim a portion of their neighborhood for water and wildness.

Ken Brunswick first saw this low ground covered in a sheet of water following a hard rain back in the spring of 1976, soon after he moved into a farmhouse on a nearby ridge. The sight of so much blue spread across the bottomland made him glad, even though he regretted the trouble for his neighbor, whose plowing would be delayed.

"Seeing all that water," Brunswick tells me when I visit him on the site of the flood a quarter of a century later, "I knew I had come to a blessed place."

The place is in Jay County, Indiana, along the border with Ohio. Lay a ruler on the straight boundary that divides the two states, slide your finger to the halfway mark, and you'll be pointing at the spot where I talk with Brunswick on a windy, sultry, voluptuous day in May.

Thanks to the glaciers, the land hereabouts is gently rolling, like a moderate sea. All over the countryside, tractors are tilling and spraying and seeding. In swales the freshly turned soil is the color of coffee grounds, but on the crowns of uplands erosion has bleached the soil to the color of whole wheat bread. Every field is backed by a stand of trees. A hardwood forest covered this region before it was cleared for farming, and the trees would come back swiftly if the fields were left fallow.

That margin of wildness drew Brunswick and his wife across the border from Ohio to start a dairy farm here in Jay County.

"I like to see something growing besides cows and crops," Brunswick tells me. He's midway through his fifties now, husky, with sun creases about the eyes, thick white hair, a gray moustache, and a ready smile. As we talk, his head swivels every time a bird flies past, and his voice pauses at every whistle and call.

"I always used to say I wanted to be an ornithologist when I grew up," Brunswick recalls. "Folks raised their eyebrows, wondering how I'd ever feed a family."

He fed his family, and fed many other families, by milking a herd of Holsteins morning and evening, seven days a week, for fifteen years— a long labor that shows in the muscles of his forearms, which are bare on this balmy day. A decade ago he gave up milking cows for restoring wetlands, first on his own farm, which we can see on a rise to the south of us, and now here on these acres that straddle Loblolly Creek. He still wears a farmer's scuffed leather boots and weathered jeans, but his khaki shirt and matching ball cap bear the logo of the Indiana Department of Natural Resources, which hired him to oversee the recovery of this marsh.

146

His affection for the sight of water gathering in pools makes him an odd character in a region where farmers have been struggling for more than a century to drain the land.

"When I was a boy," he says, "after a rain I'd beg my father to take us driving, so I could look at water standing in the fields. It seemed so bright and full of life."

The flood on his neighbor's farm in the spring of 1976 was the first of many he would see in that hollow, and in other bottomlands nearby. He began to puzzle over why water pooled after every heavy rain, even though the land had been ditched and tiled. He also began to wonder why farmers kept on planting acreage where they so often lost their crops.

That pondering led Brunswick outside into thunderstorms to watch how the water moved, up into airplanes to photograph the flooded land, into courthouses in search of maps, into libraries in search of books. What he discovered was that his farm and the surrounding area had once been part of a thirteen thousand–acre wooded swamp known as the Limberlost, and the flood-prone ground on his neighbor's farm had been a marsh. On the earliest maps the marsh was called Loblolly, from a Miami word meaning "stinking river."

"It comes from the sulfur smell of marsh gas," Brunswick explains.

At first he didn't understand why the name "Limberlost" held such power in his imagination, why the very word made him long to bring back some of the swamp. This former wetland was a legacy of the glaciers, the last of which retreated some ten thousand years ago. In its grinding passage, the ice flattened hills and filled valleys, and the torrential meltwaters at the glacier's edge carved deep channels, including one that underlies Loblolly Marsh. Outflow from these channels into the nearby Wabash River was blocked by glacial moraines, and the percolation of water underground was slowed by clay in the soil, so Limberlost Swamp filled up like a saturated sponge. Chunks of ice left behind by the retreating glacier eventually melted to form lakes and many lesser pools known as potholes. Beginning in the nineteenth century, farmers irked by all those wet spots in their fields drained them by digging trenches from the holes to nearby creeks.

While figuring out this history, Brunswick kept milking forty-five to fifty cows, morning and evening. Still he found time to summon back a bit of wetland by plugging up the outlets from three potholes on his own farm. Water soon gathered, cattails grew up along the shores, and red-winged blackbirds staked out territory on the waving stems. Next, he and his wife returned some of their fields to prairie by sowing native grasses, and they began burning one-third of the grasslands each spring. They enlisted the help of their four children to plant trees in poorly drained areas that used to be flatwoods, home to such water-tolerant species as red maple, sweet gum, pin oak, swamp chestnut oak, willow, cottonwood, tulip tree, and sycamore.

Brunswick was so pleased by the results on his own land that he began traveling about the countryside, showing his photographs and maps in schools, churches, and living rooms, anywhere people would listen, trying to persuade others to join him in restoring some of the old swamp. Although he met resistance among farmers enamored of well-drained soils, he also found support among neighbors who tingled at the mention of "Limberlost."

That word owed much of its evocative power, Brunswick soon discovered, to the books of Gene Stratton-Porter, who lived between 1889 and 1913 in the town of Geneva, a few miles north over the county line. Soon after arriving there as a young bride, Stratton-Porter became fascinated by the great Limberlost Swamp, which began not far from her doorstep. To the dismay of her husband, she set about wading through the murky waters, climbing trees, hacking trails through tangled undergrowth, often lugging a box camera and tripod and glass plates to photograph birds and moths, sometimes carrying a revolver as a precaution against vagabonds and rattlesnakes.

The name of Gene Stratton-Porter comes up so often in my conversation with Ken Brunswick as we tour the marsh that I feel there might be a third person walking with us. I imagine her striding along, a strapping, tireless woman who gazes about with intense gray eyes, a ruff of dark hair showing around the edges of a broad-brimmed hat, her legs clad in the high boots and breeches that scandalized her neighbors.

Brunswick tells me about her with the fervor of a fan. He has read the novels she wrote while living in Geneva, including *Freckles* (1904), *A Girl of the Limberlost* (1909), and *The Harvester* (1911), all of which were set in and around the swamp. But his favorites are the nature books that drew on her observations in the Limberlost, especially *What I Have Done with Birds* (1907). When Brunswick spied this volume on a shelf in the local library, he immediately settled down to read it. Within the first few pages he realized that he had read this book as a boy, sitting entranced under a walnut tree on his childhood farm. He soon made the same discovery about other Stratton-Porter books, for in his youth he had read everything he could find about birds, and birds figured in almost everything she wrote.

"I just hadn't remembered her name," Brunswick says. "And all this time, she was the reason I got excited whenever I thought about the Limberlost."

The excitement vibrates in his voice and gestures as he leads me around Loblolly Marsh, this healing fragment of the original swamp. In the mud beside another pool, we study the tracks of raccoon, fox, possum, beaver, and deer. Dragonflies patrol the surface, and bullfrogs grunt amiably along the shores. A wood duck, as brightly painted as a clown, glides among the cattails. Since every call or flutter of wings makes Brunswick pause to listen and watch, we pause often, for the marsh is exuberant with birds—song sparrows, barn swallows, killdeer, phoebes, bluebirds, red-winged blackbirds, chickadees, goldfinches, cardinals, wrens. Overhead, crows hustle about on raucous errands, a red-tailed hawk spirals upward on a thermal, and turkey vultures tilt round and round in lazy loops. All about us, the tawny stems of dry grass shimmy in the wind. The stirring in this land is like the return of feeling to a limb that was numb.

"We've still got a lot of work to do," Brunswick says. He tells me about plans for a loop trail, more native seed planting, more levees, more invitations for the water to stay.

Here along Loblolly Creek on this May morning, life trickles and sprouts and sings all around us. New grass brushes at our knees. Wind strokes our faces with pollen. On logs in the creek turtles catch the sun. We halt on the bank next to a beaver dam, an intricate weaving of sticks. The pool behind the dam rises three feet higher than the one below, and both are laced with silt from farms upstream.

"The drainage board will come through here pretty soon with a back-hoe to dig out the dam," Brunswick says, "but the beavers will rebuild it within a couple of weeks."

I can't help feeling that Gene Stratton-Porter would have rooted for the beavers. The Limberlost she relished was untamed: "[I]t was steam-ing, fetid, treacherous swamp and quagmire, filled with every danger common to the central states. . . . The muck was so spongy we sank ankle-deep, branches scratched or tore at us while logs we thought were solid let us down knee-deep."

To show me what that muck might have been like, Brunswick chooses a spot near the creek and uses a post-hole auger, twisting the long handles, to drill down through two feet of black soil until he strikes a layer of shells. "Reach down in there," he urges. And I do, thrusting my arm into the hole and feeling at the bottom the ooze of water and the sharp edges of shells, like shards of thin crockery. "I figure all those clams and snails mark the old lake floor," Brunswick says.

A lake named Engle glimmered here in the midst of Loblolly Marsh when Stratton-Porter began her expeditions into the "treacherous swamp." She would have braved mud, thickets, and mosquitoes while tramping along the shore of that lake, which dried up when the marsh was drained. In spite of the hazards, she celebrated the fecundity and beauty of the Limberlost, which appears in her books as a kind of Eden. In her literary wilderness, virtue triumphs, broken hearts heal, romance flourishes, and everywhere the waters glisten, overshadowed by trees, fringed by flowers, teeming with marvelous creatures.

During the twenty-four years Stratton-Porter lived beside the Limberlost, however, Eden was under assault. Loggers cleared the timber, selling it to furniture factories and ship-builders and barrel-makers. Roustabouts drilled wells for oil and gas. Farmers laid clay tiles and dug ditches and straightened creeks to drain the land. The great swamp vanished, and with it nearly all the plants and animals that once thrived there.

"I was horrified," Stratton-Porter recalled near the end of her life. "Drying up the springs, drying up the streams, and lowering the lake meant to exterminate the growth by running water, meant to kill the great trees which had flourished since the beginning of time around the borders of the lakes, meant to kill the vines and shrubs and bushes, the ferns and the iris and the water hyacinths, the arrowhead lilies and the rosemary and the orchids, and it meant, too, that men were madly and recklessly doing an insane thing without really understanding what they were doing."

Appalled by the loss, Stratton-Porter bought property on a northern Indiana lake, built herself a grand house with the proceeds from her novels, transplanted thousands of wildflowers onto the land, then moved there from Geneva in 1913. In her writing she left behind the image of a magnificent, luxuriant, and watery paradise.

This tantalizing image was the power Ken Brunswick rediscovered upon reading her books again as a grown man. And this was the power at work in the people who listened sympathetically to his call for reviving the swamp. One of the first allies he met was Marla Freeman. At the time of their meeting in 1990, she was a tour guide at the Limberlost State Historic Site in Geneva, leading visitors around the fourteen-room "cabin" built of white cedar logs and redwood by Gene Stratton-Porter and her husband nearly a century before.

"People who visited the cabin kept asking where the swamp was," Freeman says. "They came there expecting to see the Limberlost."

Freeman herself longed for a glimpse of those vast wetlands, for she, too, had fallen under the spell of Stratton-Porter. "I've spent nearly all my life here in Jay County, where everything seems so squared-off and cultivated," she explains, "and I never heard about the Limberlost until I read her books. It's been exciting for me to realize that right here was once this great wild area, where people could get lost, even die. Her books give me a sense of the land before it was tamed."

So when Brunswick showed up at the historic site in 1991 with his vision of the swamp reborn, Freeman was eager to help. She was then serving as president of the newly formed Friends of the Limberlost, and that group welcomed Brunswick's ideas. Together, they founded Limberlost Swamp Remembered and began raising money to buy land from farmers weary of flooded fields. Combining donations, federal money, and grants, the Friends eventually bought this low ground that Brunswick, gazing from his front porch, had so often seen covered by a sheet of water.

In the spring of 1997, Brunswick and Freeman and their colleagues in Friends of the Limberlost, all moved directly or indirectly by the writings of Gene Stratton-Porter, joined officials from the county, from the state, and from national wildlife organizations, in dedicating this property as the Loblolly Marsh Wetland Preserve. To mark the occasion, they planted a sycamore tree in memory of the giant sycamore featured in Stratton-Porter's first book, *Song of the Cardinal.*

A few years ago this land was in corn, but today the black soil bristles with native plants. The first step in turning farmland back into wetland was to plug the drain tiles and build levees. Embraced by those levees, water soon covered the low ground, but the high ground was invaded by Canada thistle and other aggressive exotics. So the next step, one that Brunswick took reluctantly, was to control the invaders by spraying with a non-persistent herbicide. Then native grasses were sown using a no-till seed drill, to avoid turning over the soil.

All around us now the dry stems of last year's foxtail, switchgrass, Indian grass, big bluestem, and little bluestem wave on the uplands, while the bright green shoots of this year's growth rise from their roots. These grasses were planted, along with a number of wildflowers—blue flag iris, purple coneflower, wild bergamot, indigo—but other plants have come back on their own, including milkweed and hemp dogbane. Brunswick speculates that seeds from some of these volunteer species may have lain dormant in the muck for the past hundred years, waiting for the corn to go away and the water to return. White swaths of boneset are blooming now, along with bold yellow wands of golden ragwort and demure white clusters of daisy fleabane.

The marsh is rousing, as if waking from a long sleep. Wherever we turn, pools of water glint with the colors of sky, yielding in the distance to meadows and shaggy woods. Broad-leafed and narrow-leafed cattails have found their way here to crowd these pools, and so have rushes, sedges, plantain, smartweed, cottonwood, and willow. The shallows teem with snails, crayfish, tadpoles, worms, midges, and countless other small fry, as Brunswick demonstrates by raking a net along the bottom and dumping the contents into a basin.

"You see why all the birds are here," he remarks.

We spend half a day together, but only tour half of the preserve, because Brunswick savors every species. The one species that does not entirely welcome the return of wetlands, he concedes, is the two-legged kind. Some local people still fear that the marsh will slow down the movement of water off their land, that it will harbor mosquitoes, that it will bring in government controls. He answers every question patiently. He points out that ditches draining water from nearby land have been kept open. He explains that the marsh breeds not only mosquitoes but also predators, from dragonflies to frogs, that keep mosquitoes in check. The people who ask these questions may see him wearing a government shirt, but they also know him as a neighbor. He answers their concerns all the more persuasively because he is a farmer himself, one who has lost crops to floods, who knows how hard it is to make a living from the land. Each year there are fewer skeptics, as the marsh recovers and as Brunswick keeps on spreading the gospel of gathered water.

Gene Stratton-Porter would have been pleased. "If men do not take active conservation measures soon," she warned, "I shall be forced to enter politics to plead for the conservation of the forests, wildflowers, the birds, and over and above everything else, the precious water on which our comfort, fertility, and life itself depend."

Ken Brunswick is too modest a man to emphasize his own role in helping to bring back a portion of the great swamp. But when I ask him if this preserve would have been established without inspiration from Stratton-Porter, he answers, "Absolutely not. She's the reason the Limberlost has survived in the minds and hearts of so many people. She's the reason there's water here now at Loblolly Marsh."

As we return to the small parking lot, a crunching of gravel signals the arrival of more visitors. Out of a rusty van climb eight kids and a teacher from a local school, here for a tour of the marsh with the man in the khaki shirt. After the introductions, Brunswick draws a lanky boy apart from the others and says, "You're big bluestem. And you two," he adds, guiding a pair of boys next to the first, "you're phosphorus and nitrogen, so you stand here beside big bluestem. Now the rest of you," he says to the remaining clump of kids, "are raindrops, way up in the clouds, and it's just about time for you to fall."

And so he begins demonstrating the water and nutrient cycles, ancient rhythms that are slowly returning to this long-used, much-loved, and richly imagined ground.

PART
3

Caring for Generations to Come

Wilderness as a Sabbath for the Land

*for Hank Lentfer and
Carolyn Servid*

*I*f you honor the Sabbath in any way, or if you respect the beliefs of those who do, or if you merely suspect there may be some wisdom bound up in this ancient practice, then you should protect wilderness. For wilderness represents in space what the Sabbath represents in time—a limit to our dominion, a refuge from the quest for power and wealth, an acknowledgment that Earth does not belong to us.

In scriptures that have inspired Christians, Muslims, and Jews, we are told to remember the Sabbath and keep it holy by making it a day of rest for ourselves, our servants, our animals, and the land. This is a day free from the tyranny of getting and spending, a day given over to the cultivation of spirit rather than the domination of matter. During the remainder of the week, busy imposing our will on things, we may mistake ourselves for gods. But on the Sabbath we recall that we are not the owners or rulers of this planet. Each of us receives life as a gift, and each of us depends for sustenance on the whole universe, the soil and water and sky and everything that breathes. The Sabbath is yet another gift to us, a respite from toil, and also a gift to the earth, which needs relief from our appetites and ambitions.

Honoring the Sabbath means to leave a portion of time unexploited, to relinquish for a spell our moneymaking, our striving, our designs. Honoring wilderness means to leave a portion of space unexploited, to leave the minerals untapped, the soils unplowed, the trees uncut, and to leave unharmed the creatures that live there. Both wilderness and Sabbath teach us humility and restraint. They call us back from our ingenious machines and our thousand schemes to dwell with full awareness in the glory of the given world. By putting us in touch with the source of things, they give us a taste of paradise.

The instruction to honor the Sabbath appears as the fourth of the commandments announced by Moses after his descent from Mount Sinai, as reported in the Book of Exodus in the Hebrew Bible:

> Remember the Sabbath day, and keep it holy. Six days you shall labor
> and do all your work. But the seventh day is a Sabbath to the Lord
> your God; you shall not do any work—you, your son or your daughter,
> your male or female slave, your livestock, or the alien resident in your
> towns. For in six days the Lord made heaven and earth, the sea, and all
> that is in them, but rested the seventh day; therefore the Lord blessed
> the Sabbath day and consecrated it. (Ex. 20:8–11; this and subsequent
> biblical quotations from the New Revised Standard Version)

If the Lord quit shaping the earth after six days, looked at what had
been made, and saw that it was very good—as chronicled in the Book
of Genesis—then who are we to keep on reshaping the earth all seven
days? On the Sabbath we are to lay down our tools, cease our labors,
and set aside our plans, so that we may enjoy the sweetness of *being*
without *doing*. On this holy day, instead of struggling to subdue the
world, we are to savor it, praise it, wonder over it, and commune with
the creator who brought the entire world into existence.

The Book of Deuteronomy provides another reason for resting on
the Sabbath: "Remember that you were a slave in the land of Egypt,
and the Lord your God brought you out from there with a mighty hand
and an outstretched arm; therefore the Lord your God commanded
you to keep the Sabbath day" (Deut. 5:12–15). By reminding the Hebrew people of their own liberation from bondage, the Sabbath calls
on them to reenact that liberation every seventh day for the benefit of
everyone and everything under their control.

Observing the Sabbath would not always have been easy for a farming people, as one can sense from another version of the commandment: "Six days you shall work, but on the seventh day you shall rest;
even in plowing time and in harvest time you shall rest" (Ex. 34:21).
A delay in plowing or harvesting might mean the difference between
a good crop and a poor one, so this was a severe discipline indeed.
When I was a boy in rural Ohio some fifty years ago, I knew farmers
who would not start a machine or harness a horse on the Sabbath, no
matter the weather or the state of their crops. Nor would they take up

saws or scythes to work by hand. The most they would do was walk the fields, scooping up handfuls of soil, inspecting corn or hay, listening for birds, all as a way of gauging the health of their place.

The link between honoring the Sabbath and honoring the earth is spelled out elsewhere in Exodus:

> For six years you shall sow your land and gather in its yield; but the seventh year you shall let it rest and lie fallow, so that the poor of your people may eat; and what they leave the wild animals may eat. You shall do the same with your vineyard, and with your olive orchard. Six days you shall do your work, but on the seventh day you shall rest, so that your ox and your donkey may have relief, and your homeborn slave and the resident alien may be refreshed. (Ex. 23:10–12)

The great gift of the Sabbath is refreshment, renewal, a return to the state of wholeness. It is medicine for soil and spirit, a healing balm.

After every seventh cycle of seven years, according to the Book of Leviticus, the people of Israel were to celebrate the fiftieth year as a jubilee, when the land must be left fallow, all debts must be forgiven, all slaves and indentured servants must be freed, and all property must be returned to its original owners. "The land shall not be sold in perpetuity," God proclaims, "for the land is mine; with me you are but aliens and tenants" (Lev. 25:23). This insistence that Earth belongs to God, not to humankind, echoes through the Bible, as in Psalm 24, which begins, "The earth is the Lord's and all that is in it, the world, and those who live in it; for he has founded it on the seas, and established it on the rivers" (Ps. 24:1–2); or in Psalm 50, where God says, "I will not accept a bull from your house, or goats from your folds. For every wild animal of the forest is mine, the cattle on a thousand hills. I know all the birds of the air, and all that moves in the field is mine. If I were hungry, I would not tell you, for the world and all that is in it is mine" (Ps. 50:9–12).

Whether celebrated every fiftieth year, every seventh year, or every seventh day, the Sabbath links an obligation to care for the poor—the

great theme of Jesus and the Hebrew prophets—with an obligation
to care for the land and all the creatures that depend on the land for
shelter and food.

According to a pair of stories in the Gospel of Luke, Jesus embraced
the liberating power of the Sabbath. Once, Jesus was teaching in a
synagogue on the Sabbath when "there appeared a woman with a spirit
that had crippled her for eighteen years. She was bent over and was
quite unable to stand up straight." Jesus spoke to her and laid his hands
on her, whereupon "she stood up straight and began praising God."
When the Pharisees took him to task for healing on the day of rest,
Jesus replied, "Does not each of you on the Sabbath untie his ox or
his donkey from the manger, and lead it away to give it water? And
ought not this woman, a daughter of Abraham whom Satan bound for
eighteen long years, be set free from this bondage on the Sabbath day?"
(Luke 13:10–16). On another occasion, after curing a man of dropsy
on the Sabbath, Jesus defended his action by asking the Pharisees, "If
one of you has a child or an ox that has fallen into a well, will you not
immediately pull it out on a Sabbath day?" (Luke 14:5).

In both stories, Jesus interpreted the Sabbath as a day for the breaking of fetters. Instead of dwelling on what was forbidden, he dwelt
on what was required—the relief of suffering, the restoring of health.
The Gospel of Mark tells of another Sabbath when the Pharisees chal-
lenged Jesus for allowing his disciples to pluck heads of grain to relieve
their hunger:

> And he said to them, "Have you never read what David did when he
> and his companions were hungry and in need of food? He entered the
> house of God, when Abiathar was high priest, and ate the bread of the
> Presence, which it is not lawful for any but the priests to eat, and he
> gave some to his companions." Then he said to them, "The Sabbath
> was made for humankind, and not humankind for the Sabbath. . . ."
> (Mark 2:25–27)

In that rousing last line, Jesus may seem to be turning the commandment on its head, yet he is actually recalling the spirit of freedom and jubilee implicit in the gift of the Sabbath. In his reading, the Sabbath becomes a foretaste of the kingdom of God, which is founded on compassion. Just as the universe, the earth, and all living things arise out of the great unfolding of God, so the Sabbath is a reminder of this marvelous generosity. It is a day for deliverance not merely from toil but from whatever entraps us.

Our traps may be physical, as in the case of disease, but they may also be social or psychological. We may be trapped by poverty or by the relentless pursuit of wealth. We may be trapped by hatred or fear, by duties or lust. We may be trapped by the delusion that the world exists to satisfy our cravings. We may be trapped by addiction to chemicals or gadgets or noise. From all of these snares, and more, the Sabbath can help to release us.

And yet for most Americans, even those who attend church or synagogue or mosque, in recent decades the Sabbath has lost much of its serenity and nearly all of its meaning. Instead of being a day set aside for reflection and renewal, it has become a time for shopping, for catching up on chores, for watching television or movies, for mowing lawns or waxing cars, for burning up gas on the highways, for eating out or sleeping in. More and more jobs keep people on duty through the weekend. More and more stores, like those on the internet, never close. Commerce and its minion, advertising, have spread around the clock, leaving scarcely any stretch of time unclaimed. In the same way, our machines and pollution have spread nearly everywhere on land and sea, leaving scarcely any stretch of Earth unclaimed.

This onslaught is squeezing out the wildness from our hearts and minds, as well as from the planet. The first word of the Sabbath commandment is *remember*—remember to rest, to limit your schemes, to relieve from toil all who depend on you. Remember that you were a slave and have been set free; remember that life itself is a gift from God; remember that Earth and its abundance belong to the Lord. Instead of remembering, we are quickly forgetting who we are, where we are, and how we ought to live.

In America today, the only lands with any chance of remaining wild are those we have deliberately chosen to protect. We need such lands, as we need respite from labor, as we need meditation and prayer, to call us back to ourselves, to remind us of who we are and of where we dwell.

On my journeys into the Boundary Waters Wilderness of northern Minnesota, my companions and I leave behind the rush of the highway, leave behind the clutter of stores, and launch our canoes into the glossy waters of Fall Lake near the town of Ely. As we paddle across to our first portage, we rock in the wake from motorboats, for gas-powered craft have recently been permitted to cruise the outermost lakes of the wilderness. The manufacturers of outboard motors, jet-skis, snowmobiles, and other loud machines are constantly pushing to open every last refuge to invasion by their products, and they are supported by people eager to use those machines, people too lazy or too addicted to power and speed to travel by means of their own muscles.

Crossing Fall Lake, we often hear the boom of radios above the snarl of engines. My companions and I talk loudly to make ourselves heard above the roar. After two portages, however, we drift into Pipestone Bay, which is free of motors, and here for the first time we're likely to see bald eagles, river otters, beavers, and other elusive creatures. In the stillness, we can hear the cries of loons, the splash of leaping fish. We can hear the lap of waves against the bows of the canoes. Here for the first time the buzz of the highway fades, our voices drop, the rhythm of our paddling slows, and we begin to see where we are.

The water is bounded on all sides by a rocky shoreline fringed green with pines and hemlocks, white with birches, yellow with poplars.

When we land, we find every crack in the granite brilliant with flowers and grass, every square foot of soil carpeted in lichens, liverworts, saplings, and moss. Bears have left black tufts of hair on the bark of trees, and raccoons have left their tracks like hieroglyphics in the damp sand. Not so long ago, this land was barren. It had been clear-cut, trapped out, mined. Then over the decades since being protected as wilderness, the land began to heal—the forest rising again, the animals returning, the streams running clear.

As we travel from lake to lake toward the heart of the Boundary Waters, I can feel my own mind running clear. By the second or third day, the frets and plans I carried from home have fallen away, and I sink into the peacefulness of this place, as into the depths of meditation or prayer. What I sense is not bland comfort, for the wind often blows in our faces as we paddle, cold rain often chills us, and mosquitoes lustily bite. Any one of us could break a leg on a portage, could go crashing over a waterfall, could spill into the water and drown. The peace of this watery wilderness is not the security and ease of a living room, a shopping mall, or any other space controlled by human beings. Wilderness restores our souls precisely because it is *not* controlled by us, because it obeys laws we did not write, because it reminds us of the vast, encompassing order that brought us into being and that moment by moment sustains us.

Even in the Boundary Waters, where every day feels like a Sabbath, my companions and I keep track of the calendar, for eventually we must go back home. As we draw near to our launching point, once again we encounter the raucous machines that are gnawing at the edges of the refuge. On the long drive to Indiana, the speed of our car over the pavement seems dizzying. The roadsides seem frantic with billboards and franchises. News from the radio speaks of a crazed and broken world I hardly recognize. Even as I slide back into my ordinary life, which is crowded with too many tasks and too many things, the peace of the wilderness lingers in me like a balm. Even if I never visit the Boundary Waters again, I am nourished by knowing it is there, following its ancient ways, unfettered, free. Every remnant of wilderness, like the Sabbath, is a reminder of our origins and our true home.

The Sabbath is one-seventh part of our days. Far less than one-seventh part of our land remains in wilderness. If we understand the lessons of restraint and liberation conveyed by the Sabbath, then we should leave alone every acre that has not already been stamped by our designs, and we should restore millions of acres that have been abused. We should build no more roads in our national forests. We should cut no more old-growth trees. We should drain no more wetlands. We should neither drill nor prospect in wildlife refuges, allowing those fragile places to be refuges in fact and not only in name. To set land free from serving us is to recognize that Earth is neither our slave nor our property.

Some people object that our economy will falter unless we open up these last scraps of wild land to moneymaking. They warn against the danger of "locking up" resources vital to our prosperity. But couldn't the same be said of the Sabbath? Why "lock up" a whole day of the week? Why spend time worshiping, why meditate or pray, when we could be using that time to produce more goods and services? If it is really true that our economy will fail unless we devote every minute and every acre to the pursuit of profit, then our economy is already doomed. For where shall we turn after the calendar and the continent have been exhausted?

Many of the politicians and industry lobbyists who call for the exploitation of our last remaining wild places also claim to be deeply religious. What sort of religion do they follow, if it places no limits on human dominion? What sort of religion do they follow, if it makes the pursuit of profit the central goal of life? If they believe in keeping the Sabbath holy, how can they reconcile this commandment with the drive to reduce every acre and every hour to human control? And if they do not believe in keeping the Sabbath, how do they pick and choose among the commandments?

To cherish wilderness does not mean that one must despise human works, any more than loving the Sabbath means that one must despise the rest of the week. Even if you do not accept the religious premise on which the Sabbath is based, as many people do not, then consider the wisdom embodied in the practice of restraint. Through honoring both Sabbath and wilderness, we renew our contact with the mystery that precedes and surrounds and upholds our lives. The Sabbath and the wilderness remind us of what is true everywhere and at all times, but which in our arrogance we keep forgetting—that we did not make the earth, that we are guests here, that we are answerable to a reality deeper and older and more sacred than our own will.

Simplicity and Sanity

he first time I assigned *Walden* in an undergraduate class, I opened our discussion of the book by asking the students for their initial reactions. A man wearing a tie-dyed T-shirt quickly raised his hand to say he was surprised that a writer as famous as Thoreau would use so many clichés. When I asked for an example, the student answered, "Like, if you don't march along with everybody else, it's because you're stepping to the beat of a different drummer. My mom's got that one on a magnet on her refrigerator."

I agreed that the different drummer must be weary by now, having been called on so many times, but I pointed out that when Thoreau used the metaphor it had been fresh and vigorous, for he had made it up. Indeed, I explained, Thoreau had made up dozens of expressions that have become part of our common awareness, if not always of our common speech, and I rattled off examples. Then another student asked me a shrewd question: In composing his memorable phrases, was Thoreau voicing ideas nobody had ever thought of before, or was he just finding new ways to convey old truths? As an aspiring young writer who had only recently fallen under the spell of Thoreau, I answered that his thinking was as original as his writing. At the time, I understood "original" to mean unprecedented, something utterly new under the sun, roughly what my students and my hip colleagues meant by "cutting-edge."

Over the years since then, having read more widely, I realized that one could find precedents for virtually all of Thoreau's central ideas—from sources close to him in space and time, such as Emerson; from sources long influential in the West, such as the Greek philosophers or the Bible; and from more remote sources that were only just beginning to reach America, such as ancient Buddhist and Hindu thought. Over those years I also came to understand that originality does not mean novelty; it means going back to origins. Thus when Emerson demands, in the opening paragraph of *Nature*, "Why should not we also enjoy an original relation to the universe?" he is exhorting us to encounter things *directly*, and not merely through scriptures or hand-me-down notions or intermediaries such as ministers or pundits. He is urging us to probe the depths of existence for ourselves, accepting nothing on hearsay or faith. The Latin root of "origin" means to rise, to give birth, to set in motion. To be original, therefore, is to seek the source from which all things rise. Thoreau was just that kind of seeker, and not only for the two years and two months he spent living beside Walden Pond, but for his entire adult life. He was original in the deepest sense, a radical, one who delved down to the roots.

I suspect that Thoreau would have felt amusement mixed with scorn for those who brag of being "cutting-edge" because they wear the latest fashions, own the latest electronic gadget, or spout the latest lingo. Novelty was never his goal; his goal was integrity. He strove for wholeness, the union of life and thought. The motive for his tireless observation, reflection, reading, and writing was not merely to gain a deeper understanding of our mysterious existence but to *practice* that understanding, to act it out, day by day. Of course he did not act out his ideas or values perfectly; no one does. But he dramatized the effort with unrivaled power. We learn of his effort from the testimony of people who knew him and from biographies, but mainly from his own account, written in one of the most compelling prose styles ever created by an American writer.

The combination of radical thinking, deliberate living, and literary brilliance has drawn countless readers to Thoreau, especially those who sense there is something profoundly wrong with the vision of the good life offered by our industrial, technological, and materialistic society. In America, one can trace a lineage of dissident souls—John Muir, Aldo Leopold, Helen and Scott Nearing, Anna and Harlan Hub-bard, Thomas Merton, Edward Abbey, Wendell Berry, Annie Dillard, and a great many others—who found in Thoreau, if not the inspiration then at least the confirmation for their own efforts at rethinking the meaning and conduct of life.

I belong to this lineage of writers inspired by Thoreau, however humble my place may be. After forty years of reading him, I am more impressed than ever by the power of his example and the vigor of his prose, and I am at times astounded by the prescience of his social critique. To illustrate his uncanny relevance to our present dilemmas, I want to examine one key element in his philosophy—the call for simplicity.

His most emphatic use of the term appears in another passage that has been excerpted on posters and refrigerator magnets, this one from the second chapter of *Walden:*

> Our life is frittered away by detail. . . . Simplicity, simplicity, simplicity! I say, let your affairs be as two or three, and not a hundred or a thousand; instead of a million count half a dozen, and keep your accounts on your thumb-nail. . . . Simplify, simplify. Instead of three meals a day, if it be necessary eat but one; instead of a hundred dishes, five; and reduce other things in proportion. . . . The nation itself, with all its so-called internal improvements, which, by the way are all external and superficial, is just such an unwieldy and overgrown establishment, cluttered with furniture and tripped up by its own traps, ruined by luxury and heedless expense, by want of calculation and a worthy aim, as the million households in the land; and the only cure for it, as for them, is in a rigid economy, a stern and more than Spartan simplicity of life and elevation of purpose. It lives too fast.

Since Thoreau wrote those lines, every threat he identified has become more acute—the multiplication of activities, the proliferation of technology, the accumulation of stuff, the accelerating pace, and the lack of any "worthy aim" for the whole frantic pursuit.

How might the embrace of simplicity counter these threats? Consider technology. Among the "internal improvements" Thoreau called into question were the telegraph and the railroad. It is an "illusion," he wrote in *Walden,* to assume that new technology, merely because it is new, represents "a positive advance":

> Our inventions are wont to be pretty toys, which distract our attention from serious things. They are but improved means to an unimproved

end, an end which it was already but too easy to arrive at; as railroads lead to Boston or New York. We are in great haste to construct a magnetic telegraph from Maine to Texas; but Maine and Texas, it may be, have nothing important to communicate.... As if the main object were to talk fast and not to talk sensibly.

Our current "pretty toys" make the telegraph and the railroad seem quaint and slow, but they raise all the more forcefully the same questions.

For example, to what extent do email and cell phones enable us to say things worth saying, and to what extent do they "distract our attention from serious things"? If the internet is used chiefly for peddling merchandise and pornography and propaganda, does it, on balance, represent a "positive advance"? If jet travel is thinning the ozone layer, burning up the last reserves of petroleum, and disturbing the climate, does it represent a net gain or loss? If television serves mainly to sell us stuff we don't need, exploiting our taste for violence and sex, and stealing our time, are we better off watching it on two hundred channels, in high definition, on flat screens the size of a wall? There is no advantage in doing something faster, or doing it on a larger scale, if it is not worth doing to begin with.

The hucksters brag that electronic media have enabled us to create an "always on" society, with stimulation on tap twenty-four hours a day. This is a comical boast, given that we dwell in a universe that has been "always on" for more than thirteen billion years, casting up an unbroken stream of miracles, from quasars to fireflies, which make sitcoms and celebrity profiles and video games seem trifling by comparison. We have traded the nonstop spectacle of nature for a shabby electronic substitute, one that requires from us less effort, less skill, less reflection or responsibility. To hold us captive inside the media bubble, the vendors of virtual "reality" must keep increasing the level of stimulation, pumping up the volume, the speed, the violence, the sex, lest we begin to wonder if life might have a purpose other than amusement.

174

In sentences immediately following the passage about simplicity quoted above, Thoreau remarks: "If we do not get out sleepers, and forge rails, and devote days and nights to the work, but go to tinkering upon our *lives* to improve *them,* who will build railroads? And if railroads are not built, how shall we get to heaven in season? But if we stay at home and mind our business, who will want railroads? We do not ride on the railroad; it rides upon us." For the word *railroad* here, one could substitute the name of virtually any coercive technology, such as television, computer, or automobile. In each case, our lives have been organized to accommodate the technology, rather than the other way around.

Anyone who has encountered an advertisement for skinny cell phones or brawny pickup trucks—which means anyone not living in a cave—realizes that our inventions are brazenly *sold* to us as pretty toys, all shiny and colorful and stylish, as if we were savages craving baubles. The principle of simplicity would urge us to resist the sales pitch and ask of any technology: What is it for? What does it enable us to do that we can't already do, and should we be doing it? Who benefits from the new technology, and who suffers? What does it displace? What skills and workers does it render obsolete? How does it affect the people who use it, the community, and the earth?

If we gave honest answers to these questions, we would build no more nuclear reactors or atomic bombs, and we would dismantle the ones we have. We would not allow snowmobiles in national parks, leaf-blowers in neighborhoods, or junk food in schools. We would quit spreading poisons on our farm fields, quit raising chickens and hogs in cages, quit injecting cows with bovine growth hormone. We would not release genetically modified organisms into the environment without thorough, long-term studies showing they are safe, and without convincing proof that they serve human wellbeing.

The standard of simplicity would also prompt us to calculate the true cost of our luxuries, whether fresh strawberries on our plates in winter or golf courses in the desert or Hummers on the highways or

McMansions in formerly cultivated fields. In another maxim that has become part of our common lore, Thoreau declared "the cost of a thing is the amount of what I will call life which is required to be exchanged for it, immediately or in the long run." The life Thoreau had in mind, as the context makes clear, is that of the individual, and certainly one could apply his metric to assess the cost, to body and soul, of buying a larger house or a fancier car, say, or of taking a Caribbean cruise. But on a planet with more than five times as many humans as there were in Thoreau's day, and with a vastly more powerful technology at our disposal, we must interpret "life" in a larger sense. We must ask, for example, how many people have been killed or maimed in Iraq in order to support our addiction to oil? How many people work in sweatshops in order to fill our stores with cheap goods? How many animals and plants die, how many species go extinct, to satisfy our appetite for lumber or coffee or beef? And by destabilizing the climate, how much suffering will our lavish way of life impose on future generations?

Americans are not alone in squandering Earth's bounty, but right now we are doing so most recklessly. With less than 5 percent of the world's population, our nation now uses some 25 percent of the nonrenewable resources consumed each year and produces over 25 percent of the greenhouse gases. We also account for half of the world's annual military expenditures, chiefly to perpetuate this extravagance. And yet, judging by the rising incidence in America of depression and other emotional disorders, by the widening gulf between the rich and the poor, the high levels of divorce, alcoholism, drug abuse, crime, and incarceration, and by the general malaise registered in poll after poll, this feverish consumption has not brought us happiness or health. Indeed, the headlong pursuit of material wealth, technological novelty, and militarism has caused grievous injury to persons and planet, as Thoreau could have predicted.

A century and a half after publication of *Walden,* what might it mean to practice simplicity? The answer will depend not only on one's values but also on one's circumstances. A middle-class American would have far different options—and obligations—than would a subsistence farmer in Peru, say, or a street peddler in India. Likewise, retirees living alone, parents rearing children, young professionals just launching their careers, and students enrolled in college might make quite different choices. So let me speak briefly of choices my wife and I have made, not because our efforts are in any way a model, but because they may suggest a few modest moves in the direction of living more simply.

Ruth and I are in our early sixties; we have been married forty years; we have reared two children and we now have three grandchildren. We both grew up in frugal households, with parents whose habits and values had been shaped by the Great Depression. Ruth is a scientist, I am a teacher and writer, and we have been employed at Indiana University throughout our careers, earning together more money than we've ever needed to spend. We have several times declined opportunities to relocate for higher salaries or trendier addresses. The first six years of our marriage, we lived in apartments, and then, soon after our first child was born, we bought a 1920s vintage house, where we have lived ever since. The house is 1,250 square feet, which was the average size of American houses in the 1950s (half a century later, the average size of new houses in America has nearly doubled, to 2,400 square feet). As many of our friends and colleagues moved to roomier digs in the suburbs, we chose to stay in our house in town, in part out of affection for neighbors and neighborhood, in part because from here we can walk to work, in part because more space for us would be more costly for Earth.

Although our house is small by middle-class American standards, we're well aware that it is a palace by comparison with the settings in which countless human beings must live. Over the years, we've made the house as energy-efficient as we could—insulating from basement to attic and sealing every crack; planting trees for summer shade; installing double-glazed windows and a high-efficiency furnace; replacing all incandescent light bulbs with compact fluorescent ones; replacing worn-out appliances, such as refrigerator and washing machine, with efficient and compact new models. And we've adjusted our habits to further reduce energy use—in winter, setting the thermostat at 58° during the night and 68° during the day, and wearing more layers of clothes; in summer, opening the windows and relying on fans for cooling, resorting to the air-conditioner only on the most sultry days; washing our clothes in cold water and drying them outdoors on a line; taking showers rather than baths, and using flow-reducing showerheads and faucets; turning off lights and appliances when they're not in use.

In our tiny yard, we have replaced all but a patch of grass with native plants, and that grass we cut with a push mower. We mix our kitchen scraps with leaves in a compost bin, and use the resulting compost on our garden, where we grow salad greens, onions, garlic, herbs, and other small-scale crops. Most of our remaining foodstuffs we buy from local and organic growers, at the farmers' market and natural foods co-op, and we eat so far as possible the produce that is in season. Most of our meals are vegetarian, and the poultry and meat that we do eat is free-range and locally grown. We do not buy bottled water, although we do filter our tap water for drinking and cooking. By recycling everything that is currently recyclable in our city, we need to put out a can of trash for the landfill only about once every six or eight weeks.

Between us, Ruth and I drive just under ten thousand miles per year (the national average for two drivers is twenty-four thousand), and the car we drive is a hybrid-electric vehicle that cruises forty-five miles on a gallon of gas (double the national average). We don't belong to a gym or a diet club, but instead we climb the stairs of our two-story house, work in our yard, do our own cleaning, and walk. Ruth gave up bicycling a few years ago, but I still ride my bike on errands around town.

The net result of these and many others actions, all as commonsensical and routine to us as tooth-brushing, is that our ecological footprint—our use of nonrenewable resources and our contribution to the release of greenhouse gases and other forms of pollution—is about half that of an average American couple, which puts Ruth and me on a par with citizens of Japan, Germany, Sweden, and other affluent but less prodigal societies. Still, our way of life is extravagant by comparison with that of most of the world's people, and it is more extravagant than the earth could support, were all of the world's people to live as we do. We try to offset the impact of our carbon emissions by purchasing shares in wind farms and other renewable energy sources, but we realize that this is a palliative, not a solution.

In order to achieve a degree of material simplicity that could be shared with the nearly seven billion humans now alive as well as with our descendants, Ruth and I would have to make more difficult choices. We might have to pay fewer visits to family and friends who live at a distance. I might have to decline all invitations for readings or lectures or meetings that require air travel. We might have to entirely forego out-of-season produce, as well as bananas, coffee, and other foods that must be shipped from great distances. We might have to unplug from the internet, cancel magazine subscriptions, quit buying books, and only borrow from the library. By moving into an apartment, we could free up our house for use by a family with children, but could we bear to leave our neighbors and garden? Could we move in with our children, or invite them to move in with us? Anyone who recognizes how thoroughly the human economy is degrading nature's economy must ponder such questions.

Our ethical dilemma is quite different from the one Thoreau faced. He did not practice simplicity because he worried about damaging the planet or depriving future generations, but because he wished to leave a broad margin to his life—a margin for exploring the countryside, for studying nature, for playing the flute and sauntering with friends, for reading and writing and thinking. After describing in *Walden* his custom of scouting the Concord landscape and imagining which farms he might buy, where he might build a house, fence a pasture, or plant an orchard, he ends by forswearing all these acquisitions and chores, because, he explains, "a man is rich in proportion to the number of things he can afford to let alone." Here, as in many instances where Thoreau exaggerated his point so as to challenge conventional views, I want to qualify his claim. I want to protest that if no one planted orchards there would be no apples, and if no one cleared pastures there would be no milk or wool. I agree, however, with his central claim, which is that we are more likely to achieve happiness by decreasing our possessions and activities than by increasing them—not reducing them to zero, but to a modest, manageable sufficiency.

One modern translation of the *Tao Te Ching* captures this insight exactly: "If you realize that you have enough, / you are truly rich." "Enough" is the key word. We live on a globe where perhaps a billion people, including most Americans, have far more than they need while some three billion people are destitute. In a just world, in a sane world, everyone would have a sufficiency, neither too much nor too little, but enough to lead a decent, healthy, secure life. Visionaries from the Buddha and Jesus to Gandhi and the Dalai Lama have called on us to work toward such a sane and just world. Like Thoreau, they have urged us to live in a materially simple way, not merely so that we might achieve happiness but so that Earth's bounty might be conserved and equitably shared.

Along with Amos and Jeremiah and other Hebrew prophets who preceded him, Jesus repeatedly warned against devoting one's life to piling up money and property. In a well-known example, a rich ruler came to Jesus and asked how he might attain eternal life. When the ruler assured Jesus that he had faithfully observed all the commandments, Jesus told him, "'One thing you still lack. Sell all that you have and distribute to the poor, and you will have treasure in heaven; and come, follow me.' But when [the ruler] heard this he became sad, for he was very rich. Jesus looking at him said, 'How hard it is for those who have riches to enter the kingdom of God! For it is easier for a camel to go through the eye of a needle than for a rich man to enter the kingdom of God'" (Luke 18:18–25). In another well-known instance, Jesus told his followers, "Do not lay up for yourselves treasures on earth, where moth and rust consume and where thieves break in and steal, but lay up for yourselves treasures in heaven. . . . For where your treasure is, there will your heart be also" (Matthew 6:19–20).

Whatever else Jesus may have meant by heaven or the kingdom of God, I hear in these terms the promise of utter fulfillment. I imagine heaven to be not a place but an experience, the bliss of realizing our true nature, as in the Buddhist and Hindu vision of nirvana. Of all the distractions that might prevent us from realizing our true nature, none is more seductive, according to Jesus, than the pursuit of worldly wealth. One need not accept this pronouncement as divine in order to recognize it as psychologically sound. If, above all other things, we treasure money and what money can buy, our lives will be given over to securing, monitoring, and protecting our hoard, like dragons defending piles of gold. The craving will consume us. Multiplied a billionfold by a global population whose numbers Jesus could not have imagined, this craving, if unchecked by ethical or cultural restraint, will consume the planet.

When Jesus reminded his followers, "Take heed, and beware of all covetousness; for a man's life does not consist in the abundance of his possessions," he was recalling the last of the Ten Commandments (Luke 12:15). Stated twice, once in the book of Exodus and once in Deuteronomy, this commandment warns us not to covet anything belonging to our neighbor. Again, whether or not one considers this instruction to be divine, one can see that it is wise. Most human strife, from divorce to war, arises from the impulse to grab what belongs to someone else. To covet is to be enslaved by greed—for possessions, sensations, status, or power.

Now consider the logic of a capitalist economy. In order for profits and businesses to perpetually grow, our appetite for whatever the businesses sell must grow perpetually as well. The purpose of advertising is to provoke in us an incessant craving for more—more style, more speed, more dialing minutes, more hamburger for a buck, more horsepower, more sex appeal, more glamour, more laughs, more thrills. Through every hour of the day, through every medium of communication, advertising proclaims: *Thou shalt covet!*

It would be difficult to exaggerate the pervasiveness of advertising. Nearly every surface is plastered with ads—bus shelters, gas pumps, the interiors of elevators, the shells of eggs in grocery stores, trays at airport security gates, room keys in motels, the paper sheets on doctors' examining tables—until the built environment begins to resemble the costumes of race car drivers, every square inch peddling some product. The internet is tattooed with ads. Our email inboxes overflow with spam as our mailboxes bulge with catalogs. Radios in some school buses now carry ads. Cell phone companies lower monthly subscription rates to customers in exchange for flooding the pocket-sized screens with ads. Public arenas carry the names of corporations. T-shirts have become moving billboards for brand names, and billboards themselves, always a blight, are becoming digital, so that commercial messages can be changed every few minutes. All of this is in addition to the tens of thousands of television ads watched by the typical viewer each year. Market researchers estimate that an American city dweller now encounters some five thousand ads, in one medium or another, each *day*. The central purpose of all these blandishments is to make you hunger for something you do not already have, make you dissatisfied with your life so you will lay out money to compensate for the lack or the flaw. Since no purchase will ever quell that dissatisfaction, you will have to keep buying, urged on by ubiquitous ads.

Along with praising greed, this marketing blitz overturns several others of the Ten Commandments, such as keeping the Sabbath holy and shunning idols and telling the truth, and it encourages nearly all seven of the deadly sins, notably pride, sloth, envy, gluttony, and lust. Advertising does not create these impulses, of course, it merely exploits them, and it does so with the best talent and technique that money can buy. How much money? In 2006, expenditures on all forms of advertising in the United States amounted to $300 billion.

There is no comparably well-funded, relentless, and pervasive influence appealing to our benevolent impulses, such as compassion, humility, generosity, prudence, fidelity, or thrift. The home might provide a counter to consumerism, but when American children spend, on average, fifteen minutes a day talking with their parents and six hours watching screens, it's clear that the family has been overshadowed by the market. By the time these children finish twelfth grade, they will have spent, on average, more hours watching television and surfing the Web than attending school. And most schools, when they are not dealing with the consequences of poverty, addiction, broken homes, child abuse, and other social pathologies, concentrate on preparing students to enter the workforce and become lifelong consumers.

Churches might be expected to counter consumerism, especially in this nation where more than three-quarters of the populace claim to be followers of Jesus. And yet, far from calling for material simplicity, many of the most vociferous Christians preach a gospel of prosperity. Televangelists assure their listeners that God wants them to be rich. Ministers in the fastest-growing churches have become entertainment impresarios whose main business is to fill their vast sanctuaries with high-paying crowds. Such ministers may swell the crowds by denouncing homosexuals or decrying abortion or vilifying welfare queens, but they are unlikely to whisper a word against recreational shopping or stock market gambling or the insatiable pursuit of wealth. I do not see how such a religion, or such an economy, can be reconciled with the teachings of Jesus.

Like Jesus, the Buddha would have seen the madness of an economy devoted to the endless expansion of desire. In his moment of enlightenment, the Buddha realized that human suffering arises from craving and clinging, since whatever we crave or cling to is bound to pass away, including the ravenous self. And so he dedicated the rest of his long life to teaching a philosophy aimed at curbing desire. He understood that our *wants* are potentially infinite, while our *needs* are few. We need nutritious food, adequate shelter, durable clothing, useful tools, medical care, companionship, intellectual stimulation, and art, all of which could be secured in a modest fashion, without jeopardizing the prospects for future generations. Once our real needs are met, we could live in peace and contentment, if we did not always yearn for something more.

Thoreau recognized this constant hankering for more as a driving force in the industrial economy of his day and as a perennial source of human misery. His title for the first and by far the longest chapter of *Walden*, "Economy," announced his intent to challenge the prevailing ways of getting and spending. In that opening chapter he examines one by one our basic needs, and he suggests how they might be met without exhausting ourselves or the world. Again and again he counters the yearning for excess with a call for frugality, as when he observes: "It is possible to invent a house still more convenient and luxurious than we have, which yet all would admit that man could not afford to pay for. Shall we always study to obtain more of these things, and not sometimes to be content with less?"

This man who was content with a diet of potatoes, rice, beans, and pond water knew that many people would regard his estimate of our basic needs as too austere: "There is a certain class of unbelievers who sometimes ask me such questions as, if I think that I can live on vegetable food alone; and to strike at the root of the matter at once,—for the root is faith,—I am accustomed to answer such, that I can live on board nails. If they cannot understand that, they cannot understand much that I have to say." Here again, if Thoreau exaggerates his austerity, it is by way of countering what he saw as the profligacy of his contemporaries. The profligacy of American society today would, I expect, have dumbfounded him, as it should dismay and dumbfound us.

To put a prettier face on our prodigal ways, apologists for consumerism have recently borrowed a key term from ecology and begun to speak of "sustainable growth" and "sustainable consumption." In ecology, a process may be legitimately described as sustainable if it can continue indefinitely without degrading or exhausting its biophysical sources. Thus a prairie is sustainable because it requires only rain, snow, sunlight, and a substrate of minerals to flourish over thousands of years. But there is no such thing as sustainable growth, not even in a prairie, where plants die back every winter and eventually decay, increasing the fertility of the soil. In nature, no organism or community of organisms expands forever; all growth is constrained by predation, climate, geology, the availability of moisture and nutrients, and by other critical factors. Thus, even the grandest trees, such as redwoods, grow only as high as sap can rise against the pull of gravity; the size of insects is limited by the weight of their exoskeletons; and the bulk of birds is limited by the physics of flight.

The model that nature provides is not one of perpetual growth, as in a capitalist economy, but of perpetual *re*growth. Up to a point, trees may be harvested from a forest, crops may be harvested from the fields, fish may be harvested from the sea, and the regenerative power of nature will replace what has been taken away. If pushed far beyond that point, however, forests give way to deserts, as in North Africa; soils become sterile, as in much of the Middle East; and fish stocks collapse, as has happened recently to dozens of species, such as cod, that were once a mainstay of the human diet. No form of consumption is sustainable, therefore, if it exceeds the capacity of a natural system to replenish itself.

Thus it is nonsense to speak of sustainable consumption of materials that do not regenerate, such as fossil fuels. Once oil, coal, or natural gas is burned, it is gone. There is no regeneration of lead, iron, zinc, gold, copper, or any other metal crucial to industry. Once a wilderness is cut up by roads, oil-drilling platforms, landing strips, and toxic dumps, it will never again be wilderness, at least not within many human genera-tions. Once the top of a mountain is stripped away to extract coal and the rubble is shoved into valleys below, the landscape will be forever deformed. Rivers may eventually flow clear if they are protected from new sources of pollution, but the pollution already dumped into the ocean has nowhere else to go. Agricultural runoff flushed down the Mississippi River has extinguished nearly all life in an area of the Gulf of Mexico that ranges from 5,000 to 8,000 square miles. More than a quarter of the world's coral reefs have already been destroyed by pollution, sedimentation, rising ocean temperatures, and the use of explosives and cyanide for collecting tropical fish.

The so-called "sinks"—the air, soils, and waters—into which we have been dumping our wastes since the beginning of the industrial revolution are finite. Their capacity to absorb and detoxify our waste is also finite, and for certain materials that capacity is effectively zero. There is no safe level for the dumping of radioactive debris, for example, or for the dumping of mercury, dioxins, PCBs, CFCs, and a slew of other industrial byproducts. Even relatively benign byproducts, such as the carbon dioxide released by the burning of fossil fuels, become dangerous when they exceed certain limits. The dynamic equilibrium of the biosphere has been created and maintained in part by biologi-cal activity, and it is the single most important factor in the continued flourishing of life on Earth. Any human activity that disturbs this dy-namic equilibrium, as by thinning the ozone layer or heating the atmo-sphere, is a threat not only to humankind but to every other species.

Near the end of his life, Thoreau observed that "most men . . . do not care for Nature and would sell their share in all her beauty, as long as they may live, for a stated sum—many for a glass of rum. Thank God, men cannot as yet fly, and lay waste the sky as well as the earth! We are safe on that side for the present. It is for the very reason that some do not care for those things that we need to continue to protect all from the vandalism of a few." The vandalism of a few is still a threat to natural beauty, as witness the push by a handful of corporations, lobbyists, and public officials to open the Arctic National Wildlife Refuge to oil drilling or to carve up the last remnants of old growth forests with logging roads. But today the vandalism of the many is the greater threat. Billions of ordinary people, obeying their appetites and the enticements of the marketplace, are laying waste to the sky as well as the land and sea.

Nature is already imposing limits on the human economy, through resource exhaustion and ecological breakdown. If humans were as wise as we claim to be in calling ourselves *Homo sapiens,* we would do voluntarily what nature will otherwise force on us. We would restrain our appetites and, over generations, reduce our population. We would fashion an economy based on needs rather than wants. We would measure every product, every technology, every private or public decision, against the standard of ecological and communal health.

As a first step in that direction, let us quit using the word *consumer* for a season, and use instead the close synonym *devourer.* Thus, the Office of Consumer Affairs would become the Office of Devourer Affairs. In schools, the study of Consumer Science, which used to be called Home Economics, would become Devourer Science. Savvy shoppers would subscribe to *Devourer Reports.* Pollsters would conduct devourer surveys. Newspapers would track the ups and downs of the devourer price index.

The point of these substitutions is not mere word play. The point is to regain a sense of what our language implies. To consume means to use up or lay waste, as fire reduces a house to rubble and ash. We should resent being called consumers, all the more so when those who apply the label suggest that they care only about our happiness and

187

wellbeing. Let us think of ourselves, instead, as conservers. For conservers, the earth is not a warehouse of disposable stuff, but the source and sustainer of life, surpassingly beautiful, worthy of love. True, we must use the earth in order to live, but we should do so gratefully, respectfully, and modestly, aiming to preserve rather than devour our planetary home. This is the ethical imperative at the heart of the call to simplicity.

Following his boast in *Walden* about a willingness to live on "board nails," if need be, Thoreau goes on to say: "For my part, I am glad to hear of experiments of this kind being tried; as that a young man tried for a fortnight to live on hard, raw corn on the ear, using his teeth for all mortar. The squirrel tribe tried the same and succeeded. The human race is interested in these experiments, though a few old women who are incapacitated for them, or who own their thirds in mills, may be alarmed." We needn't share Thoreau's prejudice against old women owning shares in mills nor his enthusiasm for emulating squirrels to recognize the value of experiments in simple living. In America, his sojourn beside Walden Pond is the most famous example of such an experiment, but there have been many others, including ones that lasted much longer.

We cannot expect to learn of experiments in simple living from the same media that promote extravagant living. But we may find stirring accounts in books, such as John Muir's *My First Summer in the Sierra* (1911), Henry Beston's *The Outermost House* (1928), Aldo Leopold's *A Sand County Almanac* (1949), Helen and Scott Nearing's *Living the Good Life* (1954), Mohandas Gandhi's *Autobiography* (1954), Wendell Berry's *The Long-Legged House* (1969), Harlan Hubbard's *Payne Hollow* (1974), Annie Dillard's *Pilgrim at Tinker Creek* (1974), Gary Snyder's *The Practice of the Wild* (1990), or William Coperthwaite's *A Handmade Life* (2002)—to name only a few books that have nourished me. We may also learn of experiments in simple living from magazines, such as *Orion* and *Resurgence,* and increasingly—and paradoxically—from the internet. There are now hundreds of websites that advocate simplicity, some of them merely exploiting the term for selling products, but many of them, such as the sites for New American Dream and The Simple Living Network, offering sound advice.

All of these testimonies to simplicity deserve to be far better known, for they point the way to a more humane and hopeful future. The way is not easy. In comparison with consumerism, the simple life requires greater effort, courage, fidelity, and imagination. In the long run, the industrial economy will undermine our ability to feed and clothe and shelter ourselves. But in the short run, it is easier to buy groceries at the supermarket than to raise them in the backyard. It is easier to hop in a car and drive to work than to bicycle there or ride the bus. It is more convenient to turn up the thermostat than to feed a woodstove or put on an extra layer of clothes. It is more convenient to buy a new gadget or garment than to mend the old one. It is easier to sink into the couch and watch a music video than to learn to play the fiddle and gather neighbors for a dance. The practice of simplicity is more strenuous than the pursuit of luxury. It is more demanding of our attention, our intelligence, our perseverance, labor, and skill.

The reward for this effort is a more gathered and meaningful and joyful life. In a letter written the year after publication of *Walden,* Thoreau mused: "To what end do I lead a simple life at all, pray? That I may teach others to simplify their lives?—and so all our lives be *simplified* merely, like an algebraic formula? Or not, rather, that I may make use of the ground I have cleared, to live more worthily and profitably?" He sought to live in a materially simple way so as to create the conditions for spiritual and intellectual richness. The root of the word *simplicity* means all of a piece, single, whole; thus it is closely aligned with the word *sanity,* the root of which means health or soundness. What generations of readers have found in Thoreau is a robust sanity, a harmony of action and values, an antidote to scatter, clutter, distraction, delusion, and sham. "To be a philosopher," he wrote in *Walden*, "is not merely to have subtle thoughts, nor even to found a school, but so to love wisdom as to live according to its dictates, a life of simplicity, independence, magnanimity, and trust. It is to solve some of the problems of life, not only theoretically, but practically."

Unlike Thoreau and his contemporaries, we now face problems that are global in scale, and so we need wise policies at the national and international level. But solutions even of global problems must begin with changes in the vision and practice of individuals. We arrived at our current predicament as a result of billions of individual choices. We can turn our civilization around and head in a new direction by making new choices, person by person, household by household, neighborhood by neighborhood, business by church by school. Beginning right now, each of us can choose to lead a materially simpler life, to conserve rather than consume, to own fewer things and give away what we don't need; we can undertake fewer activities, and those we do undertake we can pursue with more care and delight. We can move around less, and pay closer attention to our home ground. We can draw more of our food and other necessities from local sources. Instead of chasing after manufactured sensations, we can revel in nature and community. Instead of distracting ourselves with novelties, we can seek what is enduring. We can strive to be, like Thoreau, truly original, and delve down to the wellsprings of life.

We need to launch our own experiments in simplicity. Living in such a way, we will promote ecological health by reducing the demands we make on the planet; we will promote equity in the sharing of the world's goods; we will preserve natural resources and resilient ecosystems for future generations; we will achieve greater security by reducing our dependence on a fragile, corrosive global economy; we will help alleviate the poverty, hopelessness, and suffering that often lead to war. No life is perfect, but every life can become nobler, finer, saner. Just because we can't live without doing harm doesn't mean we can't do *less* harm. The world's crisis is an opportunity—to reorient our lives away from material consumption and toward inner richness, to heal ourselves as well as the planet.

Stillness

I have concluded that the whole misfortune
of men comes from a single thing, and that is their
inability to remain at rest in a room.

—BLAISE PASCAL

*T*hrough an aisle of waving woodland sunflowers and purple ironweed, I approach a cedar hut where I plan to sit quietly for a few hours, gathering the scattered pieces of myself. Resting at the foot of a hill between a meadow and a forest, surrounded by a deck and railing, the tiny cabin seems to float on the earth like a gabled houseboat the color of cinnamon. Grasshoppers lurch aside with a clatter as I move along the path, but hummingbirds and butterflies continue blithely feeding on late-summer flowers. On this last Sunday in August, here in southern Indiana the tall grasses have bent down under the weight of their seeds, the maples and syca-mores have begun to release a few crisp leaves, and the creeks have sunk into their stony troughs.

I climb the stairs and leave my sandals on the deck. The boards feel warm against the soles of my feet. The pressure of sunlight draws the fruity smell of cedar from the clapboard siding. I turn a key in the lock, swing the door inward, then hesitate on the threshold, gazing into this room where I hope to recover my balance. The two carpenters, friends of mine, who built this hut for me to use as a studio have removed the last of their tools and swept the place clean. The vacancy both attracts and daunts me. The pine floor, still unmarked, is fragrant and shiny with varnish, like a bare stage the moment before a play begins. The walls seem watchful, for they, too, are covered with planks of yellow pine, and the knots burn like a constellation of eyes.

Overcoming my wariness, I go inside, carrying with me only a pen, a journal, the clothes on my back, and the buzz in my head. I have come here in hopes of calming that buzz, the better to hear voices aside from my own. I open the windows and sit cross-legged on the floor with my back against a wall and my face to the east, where the meadow bright-ens with morning. I draw in a deep breath, let it go, and try to shed a feeling of decadence for sitting here alone, idle, on a Sunday morning.

Who would accuse me of idleness? My wife knows I am here, but she is the only one, and she urged me to come. As of one o'clock this afternoon, Ruth and I will have been married thirty-three years, and in that time our lives have been braided together so tightly, so richly, that I cannot imagine myself apart from her. And yet we both recognize my periodic need for solitude and stillness, a need that has grown more acute over the years. When Ruth senses in me the rising panic from too many commitments and too little sleep, she says, "Go, be quiet for a spell. The world will survive without you."

We arranged for the building of this hut on some land we own at the edge of a state forest a few miles from our house in town, so that I would have a place to withdraw. I realize what a privilege it is to have such a refuge, what a luxury to claim a second roof when so many people lack any shelter at all, and I do not know how long I can bear to keep it.

"Don't spoil your studio by feeling guilty," says Ruth, who has come to know my guilt all too well since the day of our wedding. She drove me out here this morning to inaugurate this quiet space, dropped me off at the end of the gravel path with a kiss and a blessing, then went on about her errands. We'll rendezvous this evening to celebrate our anniversary by sharing a meal with friends.

Although I must eventually return to house and work and a host of obligations, for a few hours, at least, nobody will disturb me. There is no telephone in this room, no television, no radio, no computer, no electrical device at all except for a light and a fan overhead. I do not switch them on, because the sun gives me all the light I need and a breeze through the windows keeps me cool. Although cars rumble past now and then on a road that skirts the far side of the meadow, they disrupt the stillness only briefly. Otherwise, I hear the chirr of cicadas and crickets, the rattle and purl of birdsong, the drumming of a woodpecker, and the trickle of these words as they run from my mind through my fingers onto the page.

Sunlight pouring through a southern window forms a bright rhomboid on the wooden floor. Even without a watch, by tracking this brilliant shape as it changes through the day I could mark noon as the moment when the corners are square. If I stayed longer, if I devoted myself to recording the dance of light over the gleaming boards, I could trace out sunrise and sunset, equinox and solstice, all the cycles of the turning year. But I will not do so, for I wish to shrug off time for a spell, to dwell in the present. I drift so often into past and future, jerked around by memory and expectation, that I lose the savor of the moment. I have come to this empty room to break free of tasks and deadlines, to cast off worry and grief.

Dust motes float lazily before me in a shaft of light, twitching as they collide with one another. I learned in freshman physics class that this perpetual shimmy is called Brownian motion, and the higher the temperature, the faster the particles move. In that same class I was also told that if you put a frog in a pot of cold water on a stove and then gradually raise the heat, the poor benighted creature will boil before it has the sense to jump out of the pot. I never tested this claim on a frog but I have come to believe that a version of it holds true for many people, including myself.

As the demands on our time and attention multiply, we move faster and faster to keep up with them, crowding our calendars, shuttling from place to place and deadline to deadline, strapping phones to our belts, carrying chores everywhere in satchels and laptops, working through lunch and supper and weekends and holidays, getting and spending twenty-four hours a day. Many of us take pills to lull us to sleep, pills to wake us up, and pills to soothe our nerves. Many of us hire strangers to raise our children, to buy presents for our loved ones, to clean our houses and cook our food. If you wish to see our own Brownian motion turned into frenzy, look at a shopping mall in the weeks before Christmas, look at the floor of a stock exchange when the opening bell rings, look at the hectoring ads on television, look at rush hour traffic. Instead of slowing down when the pace becomes frantic, we enlarge our highways and pipelines and cables, we buy gadgets and software guaranteed to help us do everything more quickly, we push down on our accelerators. Instead of deciding there's something wrong with this pot as the water roils about us, we flail our arms and thrash our legs to keep from drowning.

I have decided to climb out of the pot, which is why I've come to this empty hut on a Sunday morning. The room is four paces wide by five paces long, about twelve feet by fifteen, and open to the steep rafters overhead. All the surfaces are wood, a reminder that this place is a gift of trees. There are windows in each wall and two skylights in the ceiling. Looking east I see the meadow, a sweep of grasses polished by sun. To the south I see a grove of sycamores, a thicket of blackberries, and a field grown up in goldenrod and sunflowers and saplings. The forest begins just beyond the railing of the deck to the west, mainly oak and maple and hickory and beech, rank after rank of big trees rising up a slope into deepening shade and continuing on for several miles before yielding to the next road. Through windows in the north wall I see a welter of blowzy flowers and weeds, and a path leading to the gravel drive where Ruth dropped me off.

On a Sunday morning in town I could have worshiped with any of several dozen congregations, from staid Episcopalians to Holy Rollers, but they are all too noisy for my taste, too intent on scriptures and formulas, too eager to lasso the great mystery with words. I could have sat in silence with Buddhists or Quakers, waiting for insight, and yet even they often quarrel about the truth as soon as they rise from meditation, and over the years their arguments have led to schisms and feuds. The world is manifestly one, and each of us is part and parcel of that unity, so our quarrels about religious doctrine can only estrange us from the reality we seek.

Instead of joining any group to plumb the depths of being, I come alone to this bare space. "I need solitude for the true fulfillment that I seek," says Thomas Merton, "that of being *ordinary.*" I could not so easily name the fulfillment I seek but I know it has nothing to do with mystic transport to other realms. This everyday realm is deep and vast and subtle enough for me; I wish to live here with full awareness. There are wonders enough in rivers and hills, in libraries and laboratories and museums, in alphabets and birds, to reward a lifetime of seeking.

Although I can't let go of language entirely, as witness these lines stretching across the pages of my journal, I do manage to sit for long spells in a wakeful hush. I keep my eyes open because I wish through stillness to enter the world, not escape from it. I wish to bear in mind all the creatures that breathe, which is why I've chosen to make my retreat here within the embrace of meadow and woods. The panorama I see through the windows is hardly wilderness, and yet every blade of grass, every grasshopper, every sparrow and twig courses with a wild energy. The same energy pours through me. Although my body grows calm from sitting still, I rock slightly with the slow pulse of my heart. My ears fill with the pulse of crickets and cicadas proclaiming their desires. My breath and the clouds ride the same wind.

In his *Pensées*, Pascal remarks: "When everything is moving in the same direction and at the same speed, nothing seems to be moving, as aboard a ship. When all are moving precipitously toward excesses, none seems to be so moving. He who stops makes the mad rush of the others perceptible, as would a fixed point." Those others may decide for themselves whether their lives have sped out of control. The mad rush that concerns me is my own. By sitting still, I can measure the crazed motion of my customary days.

In those customary days, I work almost every waking hour. Even during the rare pauses—while shaving, taking a shower, waiting for the teakettle to boil, pedaling my bicycle to and from the office—I find myself compiling lists and scheduling tasks. I read as I dash from appointment to appointment, jot notes on a clipboard in the car, lug everywhere a backpack stuffed with chores. When I lie down in exhaustion at night, sleep seems like an interruption in the round of toil. So far I haven't swallowed any pills to soothe my frazzled nerves. I've resisted the sales pitches for tools designed to speed up my life. I carry neither beeper nor cell phone nor PDA, feeling already too thoroughly connected to other people's demands. And yet, so long as I'm awake I feel driven to accomplish things, to redeem the time.

Why do I keep such a frantic pace? Not to rake in more money, because my wife and I could live quite well on half of what we earn. Nor to win fame, because I recognize how small and brief my life is. Nor to secure happiness, because I realize that happiness comes to me only in the moments when I slow down. Nor to meet the expectations of a boss, because I am my own boss.

Then why the endless toil? Maybe I'm still trying to satisfy the insatiable needs of my parents that I sensed in childhood. Maybe I'm still trying to ease the ache that drove my father to drink, even though he is long since dead, and I'm struggling to relieve the dismay and anger my mother felt because of his drinking. Or it could be that I'm trying to placate the Protestant God I learned about as a boy, the stern judge who watches us every moment, recording how we use our days, a God I've tried to banish from my thoughts but who keeps burrowing back in through the mind's basement. Or perhaps, like anyone who can't help seeing damage and pain in every direction, I'm only trying to avoid the bite of conscience.

A child may take on impossible burdens, weights far too heavy for slender shoulders, out of the illusion that he or she is responsible for causing, or at least for curing, every ailment that troubles the family. Because these healing efforts are bound to fail, the child is likely to accept blame for the failure. As the child grows, the impulse to answer every cry for help may settle into a habit of the heart. Since the world is full of needs, a listening heart will hear far more cries than it can ever answer. Eventually, this child, grown up, may find himself or herself bent nearly double under the load of guilt.

At least so it has been for me. I've been spared the turmoil of war, the pain of exile, the cramp of hunger. As far as I know, I'm free of disease. No one treats me with spite or scorn. I lead a blessed life, a rarity on this suffering planet, and yet much of the time I feel torn asunder by the needs I see around me, needs that outstrip my power to respond. From the circle of my family and friends, on out through the ever larger circles of my students, my neighbors, the members of my community, the people in this country and in distant lands, and the earth itself with all its imperiled creatures, there are far more claims on my thought and compassion than I can meet.

I would not speak of this dilemma if it were only mine. I speak of it because I watch many others race again and again through the cycle of widening concern, frenzied effort, and exhaustion. Whatever the source of conscience—parents, God, solemn books, earnest friends, the dictates of biology—it is adapted to a narrower space than the one we inhabit. Limited to a small tribe or a community of a few hundred people, conscience may prompt us to serve others in a balanced and wholesome way. But when television and newspapers and the internet bring us word of dangers by the thousands and miseries by the millions and needful creatures by the billions; when pleas for help reach us around the clock through our computers and telephones and mailboxes; when aching faces greet us on every street—then conscience either goes numb or punishes us with a sense of failure.

I often lie awake at night, rehearsing the names of those I've disappointed by failing to give them all they asked. I don't say this to make myself out as a generous soul. I am hardly that; I feel defenseless rather than virtuous. The truth is that I've come to fear the claims that other beings make on me, because their numbers grow relentlessly. I wish to love my neighbor, but the neighborhood has expanded so far, and the neighbors have become so many, that my love is stretched to the breaking point. I'm tempted to run away, beyond reach of the needy voices. So I make of this hut a hiding place.

Sitting cross-legged, eyes open to this room filled with light, I ride my breath in and out as if it were the swells and troughs of a mild sea, and soon the strings of duty that bind me to the world begin to fall slack. Thoughts of the sea remind me of kayaking in Glacier Bay with my son and his fiancée and an Alaskan friend. Some days the water was choppy and we had hard going, especially into the wind. Other days the water lay as smooth and glossy as the pine floor in this room, and we glided over the surface with ease. My breath now feels like that effortless paddling.

I remember the way otters floated on their backs among the kelp beds, the way seals bobbed to the surface beside our kayaks and studied us with their dark eyes, the way humpback whales breached with a snort from their blowholes and a wave of their flukes, and I remember how the water erased all sign of their passage moments after they dove again. Even a storm tousled the sea only so long as the wind blew, leaving no mark after the sky cleared. Gradually I breathed in the equanimity of this imperturbable sea. By the end of our week in Glacier Bay, after camping each night on shore in the vicinity of bears and eating fresh salmon cooked over driftwood fires and talking under the stars with people I love, I felt as serene as those waters on the calmest days.

We began our trip home from Alaska by taking a sauna and bathing in a creek at my friend's house on an island near Juneau, a house almost as simple and not much bigger than the hut where I record these memories. He had built the cabin and its furniture with timber salvaged from the beaches of Glacier Bay. We ate food from his garden and root cellar, drank water from his cistern, relieved ourselves in his privy with a view into the dripping forest of hemlock and spruce. His place was so close in spirit to the wilderness that it left my newfound tranquility unruffled.

My son and his fiancée and I parted from my friend and flew in a shuddering single-engine plane through rain to Juneau. Already in that small airport I felt dizzy from the onslaught of noise, the blabbing televisions, the clutter of machines, the milling, fretful travelers. From there we flew to Seattle, where the crowds and racket and hard surfaces and bustling carts and droning conveyor belts seemed like the stage props of nightmare. Then we stopped over at the airport in Las Vegas around midnight, and a two-hour delay forced us to leave the plane and make our way into the pandemonium of grunting loudspeakers, maundering drinkers, clanking slot machines, and wailing sirens. I felt I had descended into bedlam. I could not fathom how this midnight delirium and the serenity of Glacier Bay belonged on the same planet. Here was a frenzy beyond anything I had ever seen, and I knew with absolute certainty that it pointed the way to madness.

Our stopover in the Las Vegas airport gave me a glimpse of life wholly cut off from nature, from community, from useful work; a life given over to the craving for thrills, quick fixes, and unearned wealth. Look at all these frogs lurching around in the pot as the water boils, I told myself.

But was my life back home so different? Was my crowded calendar, my backpack stuffed with chores, my head crammed with duties, any less crazed? What jackpot was I after? Measured against the serenity I had felt in the wilderness, my usual life seemed as hectic and frazzled as this delirium in the casino. The twin images of Las Vegas and Glacier Bay have stayed with me ever since, like the opposite poles in a force field.

The hut creaks as the boards expand in the sun, like an animal stretching as it wakes. Tonight, after the sun goes down, the joints of cedar and pine will creak again as they cool. The hummingbirds will keep darting from blossom to blossom until the cold drives them south for winter. The crickets will keep on singing day and night until the first heavy frost, and then they will carry their song with them underground. Even in the depths of winter, beneath soil frozen as hard as iron, hearts will beat in burrows, and the creek will run beneath a skin of ice. There is no absolute stillness in nature. In the nails that hold this building together, electrons whirl. Even the dead yield their substance in a ferment of decay.

As I write these words in my journal, I'm forced to acknowledge a deeper source for the frantic pace of my ordinary days. I suspect I'm trying to stave off death. If I work without ceasing, maybe death will think I'm a good boy, useful and industrious, too valuable for extinction. If I serve others all my waking hours, maybe death will pass by the ones I love. If I write books, teach classes, give speeches, donate money, lobby politicians, and march in the streets, maybe death will spare the millions of species endangered by our prodigal ways.

When I was growing up in the country, a neighbor boy warned me never to lie still for long in an open field, because the turkey vultures would spiral overhead, waiting to feast on me. Keep fidgeting, he told me, so they know you're alive. Except for rare passages of calm, I have kept fidgeting ever since.

On our drive out here this morning, Ruth and I passed a vulture that was tearing bright red strands from a possum flattened on the road. At the sound of our engine, the bird hunched protectively over its meal and thrust its beak into the bloody mess for another scrap. I found nothing gruesome in the sight, for the vulture was doing necessary work, obeying an appetite as clean and simple as gravity. This gawky black bird with its featherless head the color of blood was not death itself but only one of death's janitors. Without all the dutiful scavengers, from bacteria to wolves, our planet would be layered in corpses. Instead, the living dismantle the dead, and out of the debris new life arises.

Over the past few years, Ruth and I watched Alzheimer's disease whittle her mother to a thin reed, which finally snapped. We then winnowed down her father's possessions so that he could move into a single room, where nurses and doctors could tend his weakening heart, and we also winnowed down my mother's things so she could move from a house to an apartment. Month by month, each of our surviving parents lost certain blessings of body and mind—a range of hearing and sight, fine control of the fingers, strength of legs, precision of memory, the names of familiar things. Ruth and I have ached over this paring down, even as we know our own turn will come if we live long enough. Age strips away our powers as well as our possessions. By giving myself to this empty room, perhaps like the monk who sleeps in his coffin I am only preparing myself for an emptiness over which I will have no choice.

The Hebrew root of *sabbath* means to rest. Keeping the Sabbath holy means not only that we should rest from our own labors but also that we should grant rest to all those beings—both human and non-human—whose labor serves us. According to Moses, God went further in demanding restraint from this wandering tribe once they entered the promised land. Every seventh year the land was to be left fallow; the fields were not to be plowed and the grapevines not to be pruned; and whatever grew of itself on the land was to be left alone. Every fiftieth year, slaves were to be set free, leased property was to be restored to its original owners, and the earth was to be granted a solemn rest. Why? Because, God proclaims through Moses, "the land is mine; with me you are but aliens and tenants" (Leviticus 25:23).

These ancient rules are instructions in humility. For six days we make Creation serve our needs but on the seventh day we must leave Creation alone. We may hold title to the land but we may not claim it for our own, as if it were ours to do with as we choose. Whatever our religious views, we might do well to recover the idea of the Sabbath, not only because we could use a solemn day of rest once a week but also because Earth could use a respite from our demands.

A spider lowers itself by a thread from a rafter, settling a few inches from my outstretched feet. It's merely a smidgen of life, no bigger than a grain of rice, with a bright red dot for a body and legs so fine they're all but invisible. Even in so small a creature—and in ones much smaller, as I know from gazing through microscopes—there is room for hunger and purpose. The spider sets off across the floor, slowing at the joints between boards like a skier straddling crevasses. Against the caramel grain in the pine, the bright spark of a body glows like a burning coal. It crawls over the carcass of a ladybug, stops to examine a dead wasp, eventually trundles into a dark corner where it begins laying out the warp for a web.

The spider does not rest every seventh day, nor do the warblers singing now from the branches of a sumac just outside the window, nor do the crickets sawing away at their lovelorn tune in the grass. They pursue their passions as long as their breath holds out. They needn't be reminded to restrain themselves, for nature curbs their appetites soon enough with frost or drought or some other calamity. Among all the menagerie, it seems, we alone must be taught to curb our own appetites. We alone need reminding that the condition of our lease on the promised land is that we restrain ourselves.

The industry of the spider makes me notice the stiffness in my legs. How long have I sat here? Two hours? Three? Whenever she finishes her errands, Ruth will be coming to pick me up. I rise and stretch. The gleaming floor, so smooth, tempts my feet. I wonder for a moment if the holy Sabbath allows for dancing. Then I dance anyway, a slow and clumsy shuffle, the way a bear might dance. My feet brushing the wood make the whispery sound of a broom. Since nobody is around to hear how badly I sing, I go ahead and sing. It's a love ballad that I'll repeat for Ruth tonight when we celebrate our anniversary. At the sound of my voice, the crickets and cicadas and warblers surrounding the hut cease their chorus, but in a little while they resume, overcome by desire, and we sing together our amorous tunes.

Before long the dancing covers me in sweat. I lie on the floor, where a breeze from the windows will cool me. This room is a haven. Eventually, if I can persuade myself that it's right for us to keep this land and cabin, I'll put a table, a chair, a lamp, and a meditation cushion in here, but for now I prefer to leave it bare. The two skylights in the ceiling open onto rectangles of blue. Clouds drift across those openings, coiling and merging like foam at the confluence of rivers. Every few seconds, barn swallows wheel across, there a moment and then gone, like thoughts. Suddenly, through my framed patch of sky, two red-tailed hawks glide past. I leap to my feet and throw open the door and step onto the deck to watch them sail away beyond the rim of trees.

And so, without planning to leave my hermitage, I'm drawn outside by a pair of birds. Standing in the open air, I realize I'm hungry, I'm thirsty, and I'm eager for company. I want to see Ruth, my bride of thirty-three years. I want to walk with her through our neighborhood in the evening as lights come on in the houses. I long to hold my children and catch up on their lives. I want to share food with friends. I want to sit with my students and talk over the ancient questions. I want to walk among crowds at the farmers' market and run my hands over the melons and apples and squash. I want to do good work—not every waking hour, and not for every worthy cause, but enough work to ease some pain and bring some hope and free some beauty in a few lives. I want to carry back into my ordinary days a sense of the stillness that gathers into the shape of a life, scatters into fragments, and then gathers again.

Waiting in the sunshine, I listen to the rumble of cars approaching the hut along the blacktop road. One of those cars will bring Ruth, who will find a husband more peaceful and joyful and grateful than the one she left here this morning.

A Conservationist
Manifesto

1. The work of conservation is inspired by wonder, gratitude, reason, and love. We need all of these emotions and faculties to do the work well. But the first impulse is love—love for wild and settled places, for animals and plants, for people living now and those yet to come, for the creations of human hands and minds.

2. In our time, the work of conservation is also inspired by a sense of loss. We feel keenly the spreading of deserts, clear-cutting of forests, extinction of species, poisoning of air and water and soil, disruption of climate, and the consequent suffering of countless people. We recognize that Earth's ability to support life is being degraded by a burgeoning human population, extravagant consumption, and reckless technology. The most reckless technology is the machinery of war, which drains away vast amounts of labor and resources, distracts nations from the needs of their citizens, and wreaks havoc on both land and people.

3. The scale of devastation caused by human activity is unprecedented, and it is accelerating, spurred on by a global system of nation-states battling for advantage, and by an economic system addicted to growth and waste. So the work of conservation becomes ever more urgent. To carry on in the midst of so much loss, we must have faith that people working together can reverse the destructive trends. We must believe that our species is capable of imagining and achieving fundamental changes in our way of life.

4. Even while we respond to emergencies—keeping oil rigs out of wildlife refuges, saving farms from bulldozers—we must also work for the long-term healing of land, people, and culture. Conservation means not only protecting the relatively unscathed natural areas that survive, but also mending, so far as possible, what has been damaged. We can't undo all of the damage. No amount of effort or money, for example, will restore the roughly fifty percent of the world's coral reefs that are now dying or dead because of pollution, dynamiting, and ocean warming. But we can replant forests and prairies, reflood wetlands, clean up rivers, transform brownfields into parks, return

species to their native habitats, and leave the wildest of places alone to heal themselves.

5. The cost of such restoration is so great, and the results so uncertain, that we should make every effort to prevent the damage in the first place. Although skillful work may help, all healing ultimately depends on the self-renewing powers of nature. Our task is to understand and cooperate with those powers as fully as we can.

6. Conservation should aim to preserve the integrity and diversity of natural systems, from the local watershed to the biosphere, rather than to freeze any given landscape into some ideal condition. Nature is never fixed, but in constant flow. If we try to halt that flow, we may cause more harm than good, and we are certain to waste our energies. When we speak of ecological health, we do not refer to a static condition, but to a web of dynamic relationships. We ourselves are woven into that web, every cell in our bodies, every thought in our minds.

7. Lands, rivers, and oceans are healthy when they sustain the full range of ecological processes. Healthy wild land filters its own water and builds its own soil, as in ancient forests or unplowed prairies. Agricultural land is healthy when it is gaining rather than losing fertility, and when it leaves room for other species in woodlots and hedgerows. Whether wild or cultivated, healthy lands and seas are diverse, resilient, and beautiful.

8. Healthy villages and cities are also diverse, resilient, and beautiful. No human settlement can flourish apart from a flourishing landscape, nor can a family or an individual thrive in a ruined place. Likewise, no landscape can flourish so long as the inhabitants of that place lack the basics of a decent life—safe and adequate food and water, secure shelter, access to education and medical care, protection from violence, chances for useful work, and hope for the future.

9. Concern for ecological health and concern for social justice are therefore inseparable. Anyone who pits the good of land against the good of people, as if we could choose between them, is either ignorant or deceitful.

10. Justice and compassion require us to use Earth's bounty sparingly and to share it out equitably. For citizens in the richest nations, this will mean living more simply, satisfying our needs rather than our wants. For citizens in the poorest nations, this will mean satisfying basic needs in ways that are least harmful to the land. For all nations, this will mean slowing the growth in human population—an effort already underway with some success—and it will mean eventually reducing our numbers until we are once more in balance with Earth's carrying capacity.

11. A concern for justice also requires us to provide for everyone, regardless of location or income or race, the opportunity for contact with healthy land. All people deserve the chance to breathe clean air and drink clean water, to meet birds and butterflies, to walk among wildflowers, to glimpse the primal world of big trees and untamed rivers, rocky shores and starry nights.

12. Justice to other species requires us to preserve habitats where our fellow creatures may dwell. Through farming, fishing, hunting, and the harvesting of trees and other plants, we already use nearly half of Earth's biological production. We have no right to claim so much, let alone more. Simple gratitude to other species for the nourishment, instruction, companionship, and inspiration they have given us should be reason enough to fight for their survival. Concern for our own survival should lead us to protect the web of life by preserving a vast and robust range of habitats, from backyard gardens and schoolyard prairies to marine sanctuaries and deep wilderness.

13. Justice to future generations requires us to pass along the beauty and bounty of Earth undiminished. Our politics, economy, and media betray an almost infantile fixation on the present moment, seeking or selling instant gratification, oblivious to history. We need to develop a culture worthy of adults, one that recognizes our actions have consequences. If we take more than we need from the riches of the planet, if we drain aquifers, squander topsoil, or fish the seas bare, we are stealing from our children. If we fill dumps with toxic waste, fill

barrels with radioactive debris, spew poisons into the atmosphere and oceans, we will leave our descendants a legacy of grief. Conservation aims to avoid causing harm to our children, or their children, or to any children ever.

14. Whatever else we teach our children, we owe them an ecological education. We need to give them time outdoors, where they can meet and savor the world that humans have not made—pill bugs on a sidewalk, a swarm of tadpoles in a puddle, a tree for climbing, a sky aflame with sunset, a kiss of wind. Such contact gives promise of a lifelong joy in the presence of nature. By the time they finish school, children who have received an ecological education know in their bones that the wellbeing of people depends on the wellbeing of Earth, from the neighborhood to the watershed to the planet.

15. Whether children or adults, we take care of what we love. Our sense of moral obligation arises from a feeling of kinship. The illusion of separation—between human and non-human, rich and poor, black and white, native and stranger—is the source of our worst behavior. The awareness of kinship is the source of our best behavior.

16. Just as all people belong to the same family, regardless of the surface differences that seem to divide us, so all living things are interrelated. We depend on the integrity and services of Earth's natural systems, from enzymes in our bellies to currents in the oceans, from bees pollinating fruit trees to ozone blocking ultraviolet light.

17. The integrity we perceive in nature is our own birthright. We swim in the one and only stream of life. By recognizing that we are part of this vast, subtle, ancient order, we may be restored to wholeness. A sense of communion with other organisms, with the energies and patterns of nature, is instinctive in children, and it is available to every adult who has ever watched a bird or a cloud. A sense of solidarity not only with all things presently alive but also with generations past and to come, may free us from the confines of the private ego.

18. Recognizing that the land is a unified whole, and that human communities are inseparable from this unity, conservationists must

work across the full spectrum of habitats, from inner city to wilderness. And we must engage every segment of the population in caring for our shared home, especially those people who, by reason of poverty or the circumstances of their upbringing, have not viewed conservation as a pressing concern. In other words, conservation must be thoroughly democratic.

19. Our present economy is driven by the pursuit of private advantage. The global market sums up billions of decisions made by individuals and businesses in their own self-interest, with little regard for the common good or for ecological consequences. Therefore, we cannot expect the marketplace to protect the quality of air and water, the welfare of communities, or the survival of species, including our own.

20. As a result of the triumph of the market, the human economy is disrupting the great economy of nature. The same corporations and individuals that profit from this disruption also perpetuate it, by controlling advertising, the news and entertainment media, and much of the political system.

21. Governments and businesses promote endless growth, which is a recipe for disaster on a crowded planet. Even the slowest growth, if it continues long enough, will exhaust Earth's resources. There is no such thing as "sustainable growth." There is only sustainable *use*.

22. In order to live, we must use the earth—but we should not use it up. For the sake of our descendants, we must learn to grow food without depleting the soil, fish without exhausting the seas, draw energy from sunlight and wind and tides. We must conserve the minerals we mine and the products we manufacture, recycling them as thoroughly as a forest recycles twigs, leaves, fur, and bone.

23. Only by caring for particular places, in every watershed, can we take care of the planet. Every place needs people who will dig in, keep watch, explore the terrain, learn the animals and plants, and take responsibility for the welfare of their home ground. No matter what the legal protections on paper, no land can be safe from harm without people committed to care for it, year after year, generation after gen-

eration. All conservation, therefore, must aim at fostering an ethic of stewardship.

24. Many of the places we care for will be public—state and national forests, wildlife refuges, wilderness areas, parks. We hold these riches in common, as citizens, and we need to defend them against those who seek to plunder our public lands for the benefit of a few. In an era obsessed with private wealth, private rights, and private property, we need to reclaim a sense of our common wealth—the realm of shared gifts, resources, and skills.

25. Our common wealth includes the basic necessities of life, such as clean water. It also includes the basic grammar of life, the evolutionary information embodied in the human genome and in the genes of other species. We should modify that genetic inheritance only with the greatest care, after public deliberation, and never merely for the sake of financial profit or scientific curiosity. We should respect the genetic integrity of other species. We should guard the human genome against tampering and commercialization. These essentials of life belong to all people, and our rights in them need to be fully and forever protected.

26. Even as we defend our public lands, we must encourage good conservation practice on private land—farms, ranches, family forests, factory grounds, city lots, yards. How well these places are cared for will depend on the owners' vision and skill. While conservationists respect private property, we never forget that such property derives its protection from a framework of law, and derives its market value largely from what surrounds it. The public therefore has a legitimate interest in the condition and treatment of *all* land, including that held in private hands.

27. In the long term, we cannot protect land, either public or private, without reducing the demands we make on the earth. This means examining every aspect of our lives, from our houses and malls to the cars we drive and the food we eat, from our forms of entertainment to our fundamental values, considering in every domain how we might be more thrifty and responsible.

28. While changes in our private lives are essential, they are not sufficient. We must also insure that businesses, universities, foundations, and other institutions practice good stewardship and that governments protect the interests not merely of wealthy elites but of all people, indeed of all creatures. And we must resist the cult of violence that turns homes, workplaces, cities, and entire countries into battlefields. We must therefore engage in politics, supporting candidates and policies that are favorable to conservation and social justice and peace, opposing those that are indifferent or hostile to such causes, making our voices heard in the legislature and the marketplace.

29. If we are to succeed in reversing the current devastation, the attitudes and practices of conservation must become second nature to us, like comforting a hurt child, like planting seeds in the spring. So the aim of conservation must be more than protecting certain parcels of land, vital as that work is. The aim must be to create a culture informed by ecological understanding and compassion at all levels of society— in the minds and practices of individuals, in households, neighborhoods, factories, schools, urban planning offices, architectural and engineering firms, corporate board rooms, courthouses, legislatures, and the media.

30. In seeking a way of life that is durable, we have much to learn from those indigenous peoples who have lived in place for many generations without degrading their home. When such people are uprooted by enslavement, economic hardships, or war, they are torn away from the ground where their stories make sense. We must help them stay on their native ground, help them preserve their languages and skills, for their experience can enrich our common fund of knowledge about living wisely on Earth.

31. We cannot all be native to the places where we live, yet we can all aspire to become true inhabitants. Becoming an inhabitant means paying close attention to one's home ground, learning its ways and its needs, and taking responsibility for its welfare.

32. Conservationists also have much to learn from people who still

draw sustenance from the land—hunting, fishing, farming, ranching, gardening, logging. The most thoughtful of these people use the land respectfully, for they understand that Earth is the ultimate source of wealth.

33. If we are to foster a culture of conservation, we will need to draw on the wisdom and moral passion of religious communities. Until the past half-century, no religious tradition has had to confront the prospect of global devastation brought on by human actions, yet every tradition offers us guidance in honoring Creation. The world's religions call us away from a life of frenzied motion and consumption, teaching us to seek spiritual rather than material riches. They remind us to live with gratitude, respect, affection, and restraint.

34. If we are to foster a culture of conservation, we will also need to draw on the full spectrum of science, from astronomy to zoology. We need to know everything science can teach us about how natural systems function, and how damaged systems may be restored. We need to emulate scientists in working cooperatively across nationalities and generations, in adding to the common store of knowledge, in seeking the truth and speaking clearly.

35. Scientists, in turn, need to be guided in their research not merely by what is financially or professionally rewarding, but by what is ecologically and ethically sound—refraining, for example, from research that would turn our genetic inheritance into private property. Whether scientists or not, we should all be concerned with how science is conducted and how technology is applied, for we must all live with the results.

36. While there is much in the work of conservation that we can count—acres saved, whooping cranes hatched, oaks planted—there is much that cannot be measured in numbers. To convey the full impact of conservation, we need to tell stories, make photographs and paintings, share dances and songs. We need to listen to the people whose lives have been enlarged by a community garden, by the glimpse of

sandhill cranes flying overhead, by the spectacle of salmon returning to spawn in a free-flowing stream.

37. Every conservation project tells a story about our values, about our reasons for conserving land or buildings or skills. We should convey these stories as eloquently as we know how, in words and pictures, in ceremony and song. We draw strength from tales of good work already carried out, from the prospects for restoring landscapes and communities, from the human capacity for taking care, and from the healing energies in the universe.

38. Our largest stories are those of cosmology. Whatever tales we tell about the origin and flow of the universe, and about our place in the scheme of things, will shape our sense of how we should behave. If we imagine ourselves to be participants in a grand evolutionary story, recipients and bearers of cosmic gifts, we are more likely to feel the courage, reverence, and delight necessary for doing good work in conservation over the long haul.

39. Although conservation requires a long-term commitment and a large-scale vision, the work itself is local and intimate, rooting us in our own place, awakening us to our own time, moment by moment. It is joyful work, however hard it may be. In the face of loss, it is brave and hopeful work.

40. Conservation arises from the perennial human desire to dwell in harmony with our neighbors—those that creep and fly, those that swim and soar, those that sway on roots, as well as those that walk about on two legs. We seek to make a good and lasting home. We strive for a way of life that our descendants will look back on with gratitude, a way of life that is worthy of our magnificent planet.

For the Children

To climb these coming crests
one word to you, to
you and your children:

stay together
learn the flowers
go light

—GARY SNYDER

*Y*ou are still curled in the future, like seeds biding your time. Even though you are not yet born, I think of you often. I feel the promise of your coming the way I feel the surge of spring before it rises out of the frozen ground. What marvels await you on this wild earth! When you do rise into the light of this world, you'll be glad of your fresh eyes and ears, your nose and tongue, your sensitive fingers, for they will bring you news of a planet more wonderful and mysterious than anything I can tell you about in mere words.

Mere words are all I have, though, to speak of what I've treasured during my days, and to say what I hope you'll find when you take your turn under the sun. So I write this letter. As I write, I'm leaning against the trunk of a fat old maple in the backyard of our house here in the southern Indiana hills. It's early one April morning, and the birds are loudly courting. I'm surrounded by the pink blossoms of wild geraniums, the yellow of celandine poppies, the blue of phlox. A thunderstorm is building in the western sky, and a brisk wind is rocking the just-opened leaves. My pleasure from wind and rain, from cloud drift and bird song, from the sound of creeks tossing in their stony beds, from the company of animals and the steady presence of trees—all of that immense delight is doubled when I think of you taking pleasure one day from these same glories.

Even here in a tame backyard, Earth's energy seems prodigious. The grasses and ferns are stiff with juice. The green pushing out of every twig and stem, the song pulsing out of every throat, the light gleaming on the needles of white pines and in the bright cups of flowers, the thunder clouds massing, the wind rising—all speak of an inexhaustible power. You will feel that power in your day, surely, for nothing we do could quench it. But everything we do may affect the way that power moves and the living shapes it takes on. Will there be whales for you to watch from a bluff on the Oregon coast, as I watched with my own children? Will there be ancient redwoods and cedars and white oaks and sycamores for you to press your cheeks against? In your day, will there be monarch butterflies sipping nectar in gardens, bluebirds nesting in meadows, crayfish scuttling in creeks, spring peepers call-ing from ponds?

Because of the way my generation and those that preceded us have acted, Earth has already suffered worrisome losses—forests cut down, swamps drained, topsoil washed away, animals and plants driven to extinction, clean rivers turned foul, the very atmosphere unsettled. I can't write you this letter without acknowledging these losses, for I wish to be honest with you about my fears as well as my hopes. But I must also tell you that I believe we can change our ways, we can choose to do less harm, we can take better care of the soils and waters and air, we can make more room for all the creatures who breathe. And we are far more likely to do so if we think about the many children who will come after us, as I think about you.

I think of you as lightning cracks the horizon and thunder comes rolling in like the distant rumble of trains. When I was little, thunder-storms frightened me, so when the rumbling began, my father would wrap me in a blanket and carry me onto the porch and hold me close as the sky flashed and the air shook and the rain poured down. Safe in his arms, I soon came to love the boom and crash. So when my own two children were little, first Eva and then Jesse, I wrapped them in blankets and carried them onto the porch to watch the lightning and hear the thunder and feel the mist and smell the rain. Now I am doing the same with my grandchildren. Maybe one day a parent or grandpar-ent will hold you during a storm and then you will not only read what I'm saying but also feel it in your bones.

The smell of rain reaches me now on a wind from the west, and my skin tingles. The stout maple thrums against my back, like a thick string plucked. This old tree is tougher than I am, more supple, more durable, for it stands here in all weathers, wrapped in bark against the heat and cold, deeply rooted, drawing all it needs from dirt and air and sun. Often, when I come home feeling frazzled from the demands of the day, before I go into the house I stop here in the yard and press my hands against this maple, and I grow calm.

I hope you will find companion trees of your own, where you can hear the birds hurling their lusty cries and watch the flowers toss their bright blooms. May you climb into the branches to feel the huge body swaying beneath you and the wind brushing your face like the wings of angels.

I hope you'll be able to live in one place while you're growing up, so you'll know where home is, so you'll have a standard to measure other places by. If you live in a city or suburb, as chances are you will, I hope you'll visit parks, poke around in overgrown lots, keep an eye on the sky, and watch for the tough creatures that survive amidst the pavement and fumes. If you live where it never snows, I hope you'll be able to visit places where the snow lies deep in winter. I want you to see the world clarified by that coating of white, hear the stillness, bear the weight and cold of it, and then relish warmth all the more when you go indoors. Wherever you live, I hope you'll travel into country where the land obeys laws that people didn't make. May you visit deep forests, where you can walk all day and never hear a sound except the scurry and calls of animals and the rustle of leaves and the silken stroke of your own heart.

When I think of all the wild pleasures I wish for you, the list grows long. I want you to be able to chase fireflies as they glimmer in long grass, watch tadpoles turn into frogs in muddy pools, hear loons calling on clear lakes, glimpse deer grazing and foxes ambling, lay your fingers in the paw prints of grizzlies and wolves. I want there to be rivers you can raft down without running into dams, the water pure and filled with the colors of sky. I want you to thrill in spring and fall to the ringing calls of geese and cranes as they fly overhead. I want you to see herds of caribou following the seasons to green pastures, turtles clambering onshore to lay their eggs, alewives and salmon fighting their way upstream to spawn. And I want you to feel in these movements Earth's great age and distances, and to sense how the whole planet is bound together by a single breath.

As I sit here in this shaggy yard writing to you, I remember a favorite spot from the woods behind my childhood house in Ohio, a meadow encircled by trees and filled with long grass that turned the color of bright pennies in the fall. I loved to lie there and watch the clouds, as I'm watching the high, surly storm clouds rolling over me now. I want you to be able to lie in the grass without worrying that the kiss of the sun will poison your skin. I want you to be able to drink water from faucets and creeks, to eat fruits and vegetables straight from the soil. I want you to be safe from lightning and loneliness, from accidents and disease. I would spare you all harm if I could. But I also want you to know there are powers much older and grander than our own—earthquakes, volcanoes, tornados, thunderstorms, glaciers, floods. I pray that you will never be hurt by any of these powers, but I also pray that you will never forget them. And remember that nature is a lot bigger than our planet: it's the shaping energy that drives the whole universe, the wheeling galaxies as well as water striders, the shimmering pulsars as well as your beating heart.

Thoughts of you make me reflect soberly on how I lead my life. When I spend money, when I turn the key in my car, when I vote or refrain from voting, when I fill my head or belly with whatever's for sale, when I teach students or write books, ripples from my actions spread into the future, and sooner or later they will reach you. So I bear you in mind. I try to imagine what sort of world you will inherit. And when I forget, when I serve only my own appetite, more often than not I do something wasteful. By using up more than I need—of gas, food, wood, electricity, space—I add to the flames that are burning up the blessings I wish to preserve for you.

I worry that the choices all of us make today, in our homes and workplaces, in offices and legislatures, will leave fewer choices for you and your own children and grandchildren, fifty or a hundred years from now. By indulging our taste for luxuries, we may deprive you of necessities. Our laziness may cause you heavy labor. Our comfort may cause you pain. I worry that the world you find will be diminished from the one we enjoy.

If Earth remains a blessed place in the coming century, you'll hear crickets and locusts chirring away on summer nights. You'll hear owls hoot and whippoorwills lament. You'll smell wet rock, lilacs, new-mown hay, peppermint, lemon balm, split cedar, piles of autumn leaves. On damp mornings you'll find spider webs draped like handkerchiefs on the grass. You'll watch dragonflies zip and hover, then flash away, so fast, their wings thinner than whispers. You'll watch beavers nosing across the still waters of ponds, wild turkeys browsing in the stubble of cornfields, and snakes wriggling out of their old skins.

If we take good care in our lifetime, you'll be able to sit by the sea and watch the waves roll in, knowing that a seal or an otter may poke a sleek brown head out of the water and gaze back at you. The skies will be clear and dark enough for you to see the moon waxing and waning, the constellations gliding overhead, the Milky Way arching from horizon to horizon. The breeze will be sweet in your lungs and the rain will be innocent.

The rain has reached me now, rare drops at first, rattling the maple leaves over my head. There's scarcely a pause between lightning and thunder, and every loud crack makes me jump. It's time for me to get out from under this big old tree, and go inside to keep this paper dry. So a few more words, my darlings, and then goodbye for now.

Thinking about you draws my heart into the future. I want you to look back on those of us who lived at the beginning of the twenty-first century and know that we bore you in mind, we cared for you, and we cared for our fellow tribes—those cloaked in feathers or scales or chitin or fur, those covered in leaves and bark. One day it will be your turn to bear in mind the coming children, your turn to care for all the living tribes. The list of wild marvels I would save for you is endless. I want you to feel wonder and gratitude for the glories of Earth. I hope you'll come to feel, as I do, that we're already in paradise, right here and now.

Words of Thanks

The ideas expressed in these pages arise out of a long tradition of thought about the human place in nature, and about how we should live. My debts as a reader of this tradition are suggested, however briefly, in the notes and in the following section entitled "Further Reading."

My debts to friends for their conversation and inspiration are equally great and numerous. I have named a few of them in the dedications to individual essays. In addition, I continue to be nourished by the friendship, writing, and example of John Elder, Bill McKibben, Wendell Berry, Alison Hawthorne Deming, Richard Nelson, Ann Zwinger, Gary Nabhan, Janisse Ray, Robert Michael Pyle, John Tallmadge, Stephanie Mills, Kim Stafford, Terry Tempest Williams, and James Alexander Thom.

The two friends named in the dedication of the book—Peter Forbes and Helen Whybrow, co-founders of the Center for Whole Communities—have offered me over the past half dozen years the most sustained opportunity to think afresh about ways of leading a materially simpler and spiritually richer life. They have opened their hearts and home to me, and I thank them deeply.

I also warmly thank the individuals and organizations that gave me the chance to try out earlier versions of these essays on live audiences:

Will Rogers of the Trust for Public Land; Mary Evelyn Tucker, John Grim, and Benjamin Webb of the Forum on Religion and Ecology; Mary Margaret Sloan and Dale Penny of the Student Conservation Association; Kathleen Dean Moore and Charles Goodrich of the Spring Creek Project at Oregon State University; Frederick Swanson of the U.S. Forest Service; Dan Shilling of the Arizona Humanities Council and the Sharlot Hall Museum; Carolyn Servid and Dorik Mechau of the Island Institute; Heather Mann of the Urban Open Space Foundation; Rand Wentworth of the Land Trust Alliance; Mark Conway of The Literary Arts Institute at St. John's University; John R. Harris of the Monadnock Institute at Franklin Pierce College; Tom Potter of the Thoreau Society; Kathryn Morse and Daniel Philippon of the American Society for Environmental History; and Gerald Adelman of the Openlands Project.

I am especially grateful to Christopher Merrill and his colleagues at the University of Iowa's International Writing Program, for including me, along with visionary artists from nine nations, in a searching conversation about the commons.

Among the editors who have helped usher these essays into the world, I wish to thank in particular H. Emerson Blake, Kerry Temple, Mary Rockcastle, Douglas Burton-Christie, Debra Gwartney, Barry Lopez, Mary-Powel Thomas, Malcolm Abrams, and Robert Finch.

Finally, I wish to thank Janet Rabinowitch, director of Indiana University Press, for recognizing that an essay, like a short story or poem, is an art form in its own right, and that a collection of essays united by a concern for conservation may speak to our present condition in a timely and healing way.

Notes

p. xii   The remark by Vice President Dick Cheney dismissing the relevance of conservation to a "sound, comprehensive energy policy" is quoted in *USA Today*, May 1, 2001.

p. xiii   Senator James M. Inhofe, Republican of Oklahoma and, at the time, chair of the Environment and Public Works Committee, is the one who said that former Vice President Al Gore's proposal for a leveling-off of America's greenhouse emissions would create "economic calamity." See the *New York Times*, September 20, 2006. Senator Inhofe is also on record as claiming that global warming is a "liberal hoax."

p. 26   Thomas More, *Utopia,* ed. Richard Marius (London: J. M. Dent, 1994), p. 26. Here is the relevant passage:

> Forsooth, quoth I, your sheep that were wont to be so meek and tame and so small eaters, now, as I hear say, be become so great devourers and so wild, that they eat up and swallow down the very men themselves. They consume, destroy, and devour whole fields, houses, and cities. . . . noblemen and gentlemen, yea and certain abbots, holy men no doubt, not contenting themselves with the yearly revenues and profits that were wont to grow to their forefathers and predecessors of their lands, not being content that they live in rest and pleasure nothing profiting, yea, much annoying the weal-public, leave no ground for tillage. They enclose all into pastures; they throw down houses; they pluck down towns, and leave nothing standing but only the church to be made a sheep-house.

Notes

p. 26 Jean-Jacques Rousseau, *A Discourse on Inequality* (1755), trans. Maurice Cranston (Harmondsworth, England: Penguin, 1984), p. 109.

p. 27 Quoted by Maurice Cranston in his edition of Rousseau's *A Discourse on Inequality,* p. 180.

p. 28 David Bollier, *Silent Theft: The Private Plunder of Our Common Wealth* (New York: Routledge, 2002), p. 46.

p. 28 Vandana Shiva, *Earth Democracy: Justice, Sustainability, and Peace* (Cambridge, Mass.: South End Press, 2005); Jeremy Rifkin, *The Biotech Century* (New York: Tarcher/Putnam, 1998); Peter Barnes, *Who Owns the Sky? Our Common Assets and the Future of Capitalism* (Washington, D.C.: Island Press, 2003); Bollier, *Silent Theft;* Elinor Ostrom, *Governing the Commons: The Evolution of Institutions for Collective Action* (Cambridge, England: Cambridge University Press, 1990).

p. 31 See report from The Center on Budget and Policy Priorities: http://www.cbpp.org/8-25-04tax.htm. See also David Cay Johnston, "Big Gain for Rich Seen in Tax Cuts for Investments," the *New York Times,* April 5, 2006.

p. 33 Alexis de Tocqueville, *Democracy in America* (1835–1840), ed. Richard D. Heffner (New York: Mentor, 1956), pp. 194, 68.

p. 34 Ralph Waldo Emerson, "Self-Reliance" (1841), in *Emerson: Essays and Lectures,* ed. Joel Porte (New York: Library of America, 1983), p. 262.

p. 34 Tocqueville, *Democracy in America,* p. 149.

p. 34 Henry David Thoreau, *Walden: or, Life in the Woods* (1854), ed. J. Lyndon Shanley (Princeton, N.J.: Princeton University Press, 1973), pp. 72–73.

p. 34 Emerson, "Self-Reliance," pp. 268, 269.

p. 36 For a sampling of watershed-based educational initiatives, see Hamline University's Center for Global Environmental Education: http://www.cgee.hamline.edu/watershed/action/resources/curricula/planting.htm.

p. 39 From Justinian's Code of Civil Law, Book II, Section I, parts 1 through 4. I drew this quotation from the posting of the Code at http://www.fordham.edu/halsall/basis/535institutes.html.

p. 39 For discussion of the Public Trust Doctrine, see Mark Dowie, "In Law We Trust," *Orion* 22, no. 4 (July–Aug. 2003): 18–25.

p. 39 Paula Garcia, "*La Lucha Es Tu Herencia* (The Struggle Is Your Inheritance)," *Voices from the Earth* 5, no. 2 (Summer 2004); posted at www.sric.org/voices/2004/v5n2/NMAA.html.

p. 40 *United States v. Gerlach Live Stock Co.,* 339 U.S. 725, 744–45 (1950). Quoted in "Traditional English Common Law and Indiana Water Rights," issued by the Indiana Department of Natural Resources, and posted at www.state.in.us/nrc_dnr/lakemichigan/watquan/watquanb.htm.

p. 41   *The Autobiography of Benjamin Franklin* (1771–1790), ed. John Bigelow (Philadelphia: Lippencott, 1868; reprinted New York: Dover, 1997), p. 92.

p. 41   Tocqueville, *Democracy in America,* p. 199.

p. 43   Stephen Dunn, *Walking Light: Memoirs and Essays on Poetry* (Rochester, N.Y.: Boa Editions, 2001), p. 175.

p. 45   Rachel Carson, *Lost Worlds: The Discovered Writing of Rachel Carson* (Boston: Beacon, 1998), p. 94.

p. 55   Aldo Leopold, "Foreword," *A Sand County Almanac and Sketches Here and There* (New York: Oxford University Press, 1949; reprinted 1989), p. viii.

p. 56   N. Scott Momaday, "The Man Made of Words," in John Elder and Hertha D. Wong, eds., *Family of Earth and Sky: Indigenous Tales of Nature from Around the World* (Boston: Beacon Press, 1994), p. 296.

p. 72   Scott Russell Sanders, *Wilderness Plots* (New York: Morrow, 1983; reprinted Wooster, Ohio: Wooster Book Co., 2007), p. 76.

p. 74   Ibid., p. 61.

p. 93   Gertrude Stein, *Everybody's Autobiography* (New York: Random House, 1937), p. 289. Here is the sentence in which the unflattering phrase appears: "What was the use of my having come from Oakland it was not natural to have come from there yes write about it if I like or anything if I like but not there, there is no there there."

p. 93   Italo Calvino, *Hermit in Paris: Autobiographical Writings* (New York: Pantheon, 2003), p. 87. Calvino's visit occurred in 1959–1960.

p. 94   James Howard Kunstler, *The Geography of Nowhere* (New York: Touchstone, 1994), pp. 118–119.

p. 95   Robert Bellah et al., *Habits of the Heart: Individualism and Commitment in American Life* (Berkeley: University of California Press, 1996) and *The Good Society* (New York: Vintage, 1991); Daniel Kemmis, *Community and the Politics of Place* (Norman: University of Oklahoma Press, 1990); Robert Putnam, *Bowling Alone: The Collapse and Revival of American Community* (New York: Simon & Schuster, 1991).

p. 97   Wallace Stegner, *Where the Bluebird Sings to the Lemonade Springs* (New York: Random House, 1992), p. 205.

p. 143   Gene Stratton-Porter quoted in Rollin Patterson King, *Gene Stratton-Porter: A Lovely Light* (Chicago: Adams Press, 1979), p. 82.

p. 150   Gene Stratton-Porter, "Black Vulture," from *What I Have Done with Birds* (1907), reprinted in *Coming Through the Swamp: The Nature Writings of Gene Stratton-Porter* (Salt Lake City: University of Utah Press, 1996), p. 50.

p. 151   Gene Stratton-Porter, *Tales You Won't Believe* (Garden City, N.Y.: Doubleday, Page & Co., 1925), pp. 172–173.

Notes

p. 154   Gene Stratton-Porter, *Homing with the Birds* (New York: Doubleday, Page & Co., 1919), pp. 122–123.

p. 171   Ralph Waldo Emerson, *Nature* (1836), in Joel Porte, ed., *Emerson: Essays and Lectures* (New York: Library of America, 1983), p. 7. This line comes from the opening paragraph of Emerson's first book, which Thoreau borrowed twice from the library during his senior year at Harvard.

p. 173   Henry David Thoreau, *Walden*, ed. J. Lyndon Shanley (Princeton, N.J.: Princeton University Press, 1973), pp. 91–92.

p. 173   Ibid., p. 52.

p. 175   Ibid., p. 92.

p. 176   Ibid., p. 31.

p. 180   Ibid., p. 82.

p. 180   Lao-tzu, *Tao Te Ching*, section 33. I quote from the translation by Stephen Mitchell (New York: Harper & Row, 1988). Lin Yutang translates the same line as "He who is contented is rich" (*The Wisdom of Laotse* [New York: Modern Library, 1948], p. 176).

p. 182   The statistics in this paragraph are drawn from Louise Story, "Anywhere the Eye Can See, It's Now Likely to See an Ad," the *New York Times,* January 15, 2007, pp. A1, A14.

p. 183   Mike Reynolds, "Advertising Forecasts Call for Mild Gains," Multichannel News, December 11, 2006: http://www.multichannel.com/article/CA6398559.html.

p. 184   Thoreau, *Walden*, p. 36.

p. 184   Ibid., pp. 64–65.

p. 186   John Roach, "Gulf of Mexico 'Dead Zone' Is Size of New Jersey," *National Geographic News,* May 25, 2005: http://news.nationalgeographic.com/news/2005/05/0525_050525_deadzone.html.

p. 186   Joshua Reichert, "The Death of Coral Reefs," *San Francisco Chronicle,* July 20, 2001: http://www.sfgate.com/cgi-bin/article.cgi?file=/chronicle/archive/2001/07/20/ED93305.DTL.

p. 186   The entry is for January 3, 1861, and is quoted here from Bradford Torrey and Francis H. Allen, eds., *The Journal of Henry David Thoreau,* Vol. XIV (Salt Lake City: Peregrine Smith, 1984), pp. 306–307.

p. 188   Thoreau, *Walden*, p. 65.

p. 189   Henry David Thoreau, *Letters to a Spiritual Seeker,* ed. Bradley P. Dean (New York: Norton, 2004), p. 125.

p. 190   Thoreau, *Walden*, pp. 14–15.

p. 193   Blaise Pascal, *Selections from the Thoughts,* trans. and ed. Arthur H. Beattie (Arlington Heights, Ill.: AHM, 1965), p. 34.

p. 198   Thomas Merton, *The Intimate Journals* (San Francisco: HarperCollins, 1999), p. 108.

p. 199   Pascal, *Selections from the Thoughts,* p. 53.
p. 221   Gary Snyder, "For the Children," *No Nature: New and Selected Poems* (New York: Pantheon, 1994), p. 259.

Further Reading

Here are a few essential books that help us understand how we fit into the blooming, buzzing, burgeoning web of life, and how to care for the earth. In an effort to keep the list short enough to be useful, I have limited myself to twenty titles, all by American authors, all prose nonfiction. These self-imposed restrictions have forced me to exclude many books that I treasure. The list is arranged chronologically by date of publication, because these books record an evolving conversation, about who we are, where we are, and how we ought to live.

Henry David Thoreau, *Walden: or, Life in the Woods* (1854)
John Muir, *The Mountains of California* (1894)
Mary Austin, *The Land of Little Rain* (1903)
Henry Beston, *The Outermost House* (1928)
Aldo Leopold, *A Sand County Almanac and
    Sketches Here and There* (1949)
Loren Eiseley, *The Immense Journey* (1957)
John Hay, *The Run* (1959)
Rachel Carson, *Silent Spring* (1962)
Edward Abbey, *Desert Solitaire: A Season in the Wilderness* (1968)
Wallace Stegner, *The Sound of Mountain Water* (1969)
Ann Zwinger, *Beyond the Aspen Grove* (1970)
Annie Dillard, *Pilgrim at Tinker Creek* (1974)
Wendell Berry, *The Unsettling of America: Culture and Agriculture* (1977)
Peter Matthiessen, *The Snow Leopard* (1978)
Edward O. Wilson, *Biophilia: The Human Bond with Other Species* (1984)
Barry Lopez, *Arctic Dreams: Imagination and Desire in a
    Northern Landscape* (1986)

Further Reading

Bill McKibben, *The End of Nature* (1989)
Gary Snyder, *The Practice of the Wild* (1990)
Terry Tempest Williams, *Refuge: An Unnatural History
of Family and Place* (1991)
Thomas Berry and Brian Swimme, *The Universe Story* (1992)

For a more comprehensive sampling of this immense literature, consult these two invaluable anthologies:

John Elder and Robert Finch, eds., *Nature Writing:
The Tradition in English* (2002)
Bill McKibben, ed., *American Earth: Environmental
Writing Since Thoreau* (2008)

SCOTT RUSSELL SANDERS, Distinguished Professor of English at Indiana University, Bloomington, is the author of twenty books of fiction and nonfiction, including the following Indiana University Press titles: *Writing from the Center, Terrarium, Bad Man Ballad, Stone Country* (co-authored with Jeffrey Wolin), *Bloomington Past and Present* (co-authored with James Madison and Will Counts), and *Audubon Reader* (editor). Winner of the Lannan Literary Award, the John Burroughs Essay Award, the Mark Twain Award, and the AWP Award in Creative Non-fiction, Sanders has received fellowships in support of his writing from the Guggenheim Foundation and the National Endowment for the Arts.

green
press
INITIATIVE

Indiana University Press is committed to preserving ancient forests and natural resources. We elected to print this title on 30% postconsumer recycled paper, processed chlorine-free. As a result, for this printing, we have saved:

3 Trees (40' tall and 6-8" diameter)
992 Gallons of Wastewater
2 million BTUs of Total Energy
127 Pounds of Solid Waste
239 Pounds of Greenhouse Gases

Indiana University Press made this paper choice because our printer, Thomson-Shore, Inc., is a member of Green Press Initiative, a nonprofit program dedicated to supporting authors, publishers, and suppliers in their efforts to reduce their use of fiber obtained from endangered forests.

For more information, visit www.greenpressinitiative.org

Environmental impact estimates were made using the Environmental Defense Paper Calculator. For more information visit: www.edf.org/papercalculator